illumination
Young Adult Bible Studies

STEPHEN CHEYNEY

Illumination
Young Adult Bible Studies

© 2013 Stephen R. Cheyney. All rights reserved.
ISBN 978-0-9889559-0-5

The Scripture quotations contained herein [unless otherwise noted] are from the New Revised Standard Version Bible, copyright © 1989 by the Division of Christian Education of the National Council of the Churches of Christ in the U.S.A. Used by permission. All rights reserved.

Scripture quotations marked CEV are taken from the Contemporary English Version © 1995, American Bible Society.

Scripture quotations from THE MESSAGE. Copyright © by Eugene H. Peterson 1993, 1994, 1995, 1996, 2000, 2001, 2002. Used by permission of NavPress Publishing Group.

CONTENTS

INTRODUCTION

FORMING GROUPS
This book can be read for personal growth. However, the book has been designed for small groups. One possible strategy is to invite three friends to join you in a small group that meets weekly. Then ask each of these friends to invite one other person. Now as a group of seven you can begin your journey through the eighteen chapters of this book.

Groups may want to take eighteen weeks to run through this Bible study. Or you can use it on weekend retreats, mission trips and many other settings.

SCRATCH THE SURFACE OR GO DEEP
I originally designed this book as a small group curriculum for the college students I work with. With this book I want my students to dive into deep theological themes but I also realize they are overwhelmed with classes, working and staying busy.

So the way I designed this book is to bring up theological themes that you can explore deeply. However, if time isn't available for such an exploration, at least I have scratched the surface of various theological topics that many avoid.

Of course people of all ages can certainly use this book. And as a Bible study, I wouldn't expect you to read it cover to cover. Each chapter is based on a piece of Scripture identified at the beginning. Each chapter also has different sections including group questions at the end.

CHAPTER 1

God is a Gift Giver

SCRIPTURE

Read Matthew 16:13-20

FIRST THINGS

We've all met someone who seems to have God figured out. At least that's the way it seams. They may know how to pray really well. They are good at making their voice deeper in religious settings. They may know how to dress like the latest hipster Christian or at least believe Christians have some sort of dress code. They may have a swagger about them that radiates their closeness with God. Yet, I hope I'm not like this. I don't think so. Really I have enough trouble figuring myself out, let alone God. I misread people all the time. I misread my own feelings more often than not. I have trouble listening to my gut. So, its safe to say that I probably misread God. Often.

In fact, no one has God cornered.

> What are some common beliefs the church has taught you about who Jesus is?

....

....

....

STUDY

Matthew 16:13-20 is the Synoptic account commonly known as Peter's confession. The account begins with Jesus bluntly asking his disciples "Who do people say that the Son of Man is?" After a few responses Jesus then adjusts the question: "But who do you say that I am?" Simon Peter replied, "the Messiah, the Son of the living God."

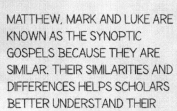

SYNOPTIC

MATTHEW, MARK AND LUKE ARE KNOWN AS THE SYNOPTIC GOSPELS BECAUSE THEY ARE SIMILAR. THEIR SIMILARITIES AND DIFFERENCES HELPS SCHOLARS BETTER UNDERSTAND THEIR CONTEXT AND NATURE.

In a literary sense, this is the climax of the Gospel of Matthew. The entire Gospel hinges on this simple, yet complex statement by Peter. It remains dramatic in the sense that our own confession of Jesus is equally as significant. When we get lazy or tired we sometimes toss around confessions like Peter's. We may say Jesus is Lord or Jesus is our savior. These answers may be right, but when we say this without thought or consideration, our words become creeds of apathy. And to say Jesus is Lord should be anything but apathetic.

Notice that Jesus pressed the disciples for their own belief. What others say about Jesus was and remains important, but here Jesus asks for a more reflective answer. Here Jesus wasn't concerned with dogma or theological statements. It's obvious to me that Jesus wanted to distinguish between what others say about him and what we say or feel about him. Jesus wanted to know the personal convictions of his disciples. He wanted to know them.

Orthodoxy means having the right opinion. Some churches live and die by orthodoxy. For these churches you have to think and speak like them.

To be orthodox is to share their opinion. So in their eyes, your thoughts and your God talk must be right. But I'm convinced life isn't that easy. Actually, it didn't matter to Jesus what others believed. Jesus wasn't quizzing his disciples' orthodoxy. Jesus wanted to know where he stood among his disciples.

> Where does Jesus stand among you?

....

....

....

If we believe Jesus is the Messiah then our belief should inspire us to model that belief to others. However, modeling Jesus' messianic nature is a bit odd. We call Jesus the Messiah because he is the anointed one. To be anointed was to be given political power. It's like saying Jesus should be president.[1] For Peter, Jesus' status as Messiah signifies his trust in God that finally Israel can be restored ... politically.

While this concept may have worked for Peter, living and walking with Jesus in a dangerous political environment, one wonders what weight Jesus' messianic nature holds today? Holding additional beliefs about Jesus might help us frame his nature and shape our lives. For example, I believe God is a gift giver. As far as I can tell, this is not an inherent assumption with messiahship. Nonetheless, God gives gifts. Actually this isn't an inherent belief at all. When a hurricane or earthquake hits, most people don't reflect on the gifts God has given. As a person drinks himself to bed, he probably doesn't reflect on his gifts from God. When a

---

[1] See Shane Claiborne & Chris Haw. Jesus for President.

college girl gets a call that her dad had a heart attack, she probably doesn't count her God given gifts. Yet, despite the problems of life, God is a gift giver. In good times we can buy this argument. In bad times, we might have to just hang on to this notion. But it's also okay to doubt it. From what I discerned about God, God gives gifts without regard to our acceptance of them.

Everything we have is a gift. Our breath and life – they are gifts. Our uniqueness and personality – gifts. We have all been gifted. Paul, when teaching about spiritual gifts, writes, "the Spirit has given each of us a special way of serving others (1 Corinthians 12:7, CEV)." What this means is that not only does God gift us, these same gifts are meant for the good of the world. So, we ought not to ignore these gifts.

One gift God gives us is the gift of love. I've encountered people who feel an absence from God's love. They feel alone or abandoned. Many of us have felt this way usually because our faith depends on feeling or seeing God. When we base our faith on the obstacles around us – say feeling unloved, alone, unworthy or unacceptable – then we ignore the presence of love we can't see or grasp. But Paul teaches that we are grounded in a love that surrounds us from every direction (Ephesians 3:17). So, even when we don't feel, see or experience the love of God, it is still present. That alone is something to embrace.

> Jot down a time when you felt God really loved you.

God also gives us readiness. It's a readiness to make a difference in the world. The Bible might call this sanctification or becoming holy. Jesus sends us, like his first disciples, into the world to "cure the sick, raise the dead, cleanse the lepers, [and] cast out demons (Matthew 10:8)." And as Jesus sends us, he sends us ready. My favorite quote in the Message, Eugene Peterson's paraphrase of the Bible, is his take on Matthew 10:9, when he writes, "You don't need a lot of equipment. You are the equipment." In other words, God gives us a readiness for mission and life and sanctifies us, or fully equips us for what's ahead.

> How has God equipped you?

God also gives us a family. I don't mean a modern family with two dads, a mentally ill stepsister, and a forty-five year-old uncle who lives in the basement that he refers to as the undercroft. You might have that family as well. Instead, I simply mean that God has given us one another. As children of God we are all brothers and sisters. And as brothers and sisters we are called to live in community as if we were part of a family. While it's hard enough to tolerate life with our own relatives, Jesus calls us to bear the fruits of life with everyone. Ephesians 2:19 says it well in that we "are no longer strangers and aliens, but ... citizens with the saints and also members of the household of God."

> Who will you pull closer as your new brothers and sisters?

....

....

....

QUESTIONS

> Compare Matthew 16:13-20 to Mark 8:27-30 and Luke 9:18-21. Discuss the idea of the Synoptic Gospels.

> Review the questions and responses from this session. Ask for participants to share.

> Try to have the group make a comprehensive list of various ways to describe Jesus. After you can think of no more, have the group narrow down the list. Have them strike though each title one-by-one until the list is reduced to one. Once finished, reflect on this final attribute chosen by the group. Also discuss how this process felt to group members.

> Challenge the group to work together for a common mission. Since this is the first session, collectively decide on a project or task that can be accomplished by the group by the end of the sessions.

CHAPTER 2

Called to Ministry

....

SCRIPTURE

Read Romans 12:9-21

FIRST THINGS

Martin Luther's works gave fame to the phrase "priesthood of all believers" when he wrote that our baptism consecrate us as priests. It's the notion that all Christians are priests – ministers within God's kingdom. Luther was adamant about bridging the gap between those who claimed closeness to God and those who couldn't. He fought for equal access to the Scripture and believed that God was revealed only in Jesus Christ. Not priests. While this is a hallmark of the protestant reformation, still today some five hundred years later, people still feel gapped from God.

> Reflect on Martin Luther's claim that there exists a "priesthood of all believers." Show some signs of this reality from your own life.

....

....

....

STUDY

In this section of Paul's letter to Rome, he focuses on human behavior and particularly relationships. Paul addresses real world stuff like conflict and anger, respect and sharing and the practical ways we can live our faith.

We all encounter people with real problems. Christians, Jews, Muslims and others at times have faiths that are strong and at times weak. Despite what Jesus teaches us about worry, we meet Christians who worry and doubt. We find eternally optimistic folks who always seem to lift up others. And we also encounter the defeatist downers who always seem to stop the cheer. These ranges of human emotion are natural and universal. However, you will also find many unnatural emotions as well. Fake smiles, courtesy laughs and being who you are not rate high among the possibilities. We are really good at faking it.

Yet, Paul says "let love be genuine."

The absolute best impersonator I've ever come across is a student I know in Charlotte. Ben can impersonate Harry Carey, Bill Clinton, George W. Bush, Bill Cosby and pretty much whomever you ask him to impersonate. His raw talent is amazing. Ben's humor is incredibly alluring. But even more so, I'm afraid, is the seductive drawl of trying to be someone you're not. Ben's impersonating for fun, but we know plenty of people who impersonate as their subtle withdrawal from their own self-worth. I'm fairly certain this habit isn't intentional. We just set aside genuineness and instead opt for the art of masking. Yet, when God started to make the world, and all of us, God affirmed its goodness.

And Paul says, "hold fast to what is good."

The scandalous nature of the life of Jesus is that he didn't pretend to be who he wasn't. The crowds asked for a tyrant to replace the tyranny of

Rome, but Jesus remained weak. As Paul teaches the church in Rome to be, Jesus was also "patient in suffering." In fact, all that Paul claims we need for a practical faith in Romans 12 are attributes of Jesus himself: He blessed those who persecuted him, he wept with those who wept, he was not haughty and he associated with the oppressed. Jesus was real, to himself and to the world.

> How scandalous would it be to live genuinely?

....

....

....

As Luther taught, we are part of a royal priesthood of believers. He bases this mostly on the letters of Peter. However, Paul alludes to this as well when he asks his reader to "contribute to the saints; extend hospitality to strangers (Romans 12:13)." The Greek *koinoneo*, which is translated here as "contribute," has the holistic nature of both sharing and serving. In other words, we could just as easily translate this verse "minister to the saints; extend hospitality to strangers." Hence, the act of giving is, in fact, ministry.

> List some times when you have shared or served, and thus ministered:

....

....

....

Perhaps the most important responsibility for the Christian is the service of hospitality. Paul says "extend hospitality to strangers." It's startling to think that a modern day hostel may adhere to the Scripture better than a church. When I go to the YMCA I can swim, climb the rock wall, play basketball, get on the treadmill or lift weights. However, I can't stay overnight. It didn't used to be this way. The market has trumped the YMCA's storied history of hospitality. Likewise, when I step into a church sometimes I see signs that point to a "welcome center." However, Paul calls the entire body of Christ to be a center of welcome. Not a kiosk.

> List some ways you can stop kiosking your hospitality and instead really welcome strangers.

....

....

....

Obviously, conflict is part of life. Students butt heads with professors. Customers argue with managers. Congress fights the president. Strife and conflict abound. Life is a pressure cooker and when people are placed under pressure we tend to boil. In many ways it's disparaging to think that Paul can blindly say, "live in harmony with one another." Sometimes I ask myself, what does he know? However, the fact that Paul writes these words should mean a lot. He certainly lived the checkered past as being both the villain and the vilified. Paul's words are not religious jargon. He's speaking wisdom straight from experience. In conflict or debate, our natural instinct is to blame others. But Paul suggests that we look at our own actions instead.

> Step Eight of the 12 Steps of Alcoholics Anonymous is to make amends to the people we have harmed. Where would you start?

....

....

....

> How can the body of Christ apply Romans 12 to the conflict between the people of Darfur and the Janjaweed? Or wherever?

....

....

....

> How can the body of Christ apply Romans 12 to Congress or the school board?

....

....

....

> How can the body of Christ apply Romans 12 to communities who rail against mixed-income housing?

....

....

....

QUESTIONS

➢ Have an impersonation contest. Before the time starts, take a sheet of paper and write out ten or so names of famous people. Have participants draw names and attempt to impersonate their character.

➢ Review the session individual questions. Ask for participants to share.

➢ Share with the group the Twelve Steps of Alcoholics Anonymous. Have them reflect on these steps and how they may apply to anyone.

➢ Review the common mission or task the group decided on and discuss its execution.

CHAPTER 3

Managing Conflict

SCRIPTURE

Read Matthew 18:15-20

FIRST THINGS

I have a friend who recalls his first thoughts of God as being like a creepy voyeur. His concept of God began when he started to date. Anytime he went out on a date, his parents would tell him "God is watching." Perhaps, it was their parental way of telling him "be strong because God is with you." But we are convinced it was their way of trying to keep his hands to himself and his teenage body fully clothed. So, with any sly move, they may have been telling him, "God will see." Growing up Will didn't appreciate this peeping God interrupting his date nights. This image of God actually stuck.

> How do you think God watches our lives?

_____

_____

_____

STUDY

In Matthew 18 Jesus establishes a principle of conflict management that is unique but often misunderstood. The first mistake we usually make with this passage is how we define sin. It is important to note that in this text no particular sin has been identified. Matthew 18:15 begins simply "if another sins against you, go…" Here the onus of the infliction is ours. Not only that, Jesus is using the word sin in a very general sense, which teaches us something about the very nature of sin itself.

First of all, just to be clear, a good way to understand sin is just to associate sin with humanity. Yes we have great human attributes. Yes God has gifted us. And yes we were created in the image of God. However, we all are afflicted and conflicted by sin really because we are human, not God. Sin is our human condition. You can try to live sin free, and that's important, but if you are human, you can't brush sin off that easily. Just read Romans 3:23. We all sin.

But there is something sneaky about sin that I've found many people have never considered. It turns out that sin can be both individual and corporate.

Think of my friend Will in the car with his date. His parents were worried about the individual sins he might commit. That's one type of sin. Easy to identify, label, name and sometimes deal with. In this case, if Will sinned, God would know. This is the most preferred use of the word sin in the Hebrew Bible. Here sin can be summed up as a violation of the law: You done bad.

But individual sin has a brother who is a bit more elusive. More often than not, the New Testament views sin as a condition of our brokenness and this brokenness is corporate. This corporate sin is like owning a share of a large amount of law breaking. We are all stakeholders in sin that has other investors. For example, when America drops a bomb, all of its citizens are responsible for its devastation, not just the pilot. We all share in its destructive capability. Same goes with how we shop or what we drive. In fact, most of our sin is corporate.

Corporate sin is like a food chain. A food chain exemplifies cause and effect from say grass to grasshopper, and so forth. Corporate sin, then, reminds us that it is impossible to escape the reality of our brokenness. No matter how good we are, no matter how well we observe the commandments and the laws, we share in the investment of our brokenness. Our humanness links our sin with the sin of others.

Matthew 18 helps to remind us that no matter how much we do to avoid sin, it keeps showing up again and again.

> I gave an example of a dropping a bomb as corporate sin. Give your own "chain of sin" example:

So lets say that someone has "sinned against you." You feel wronged. A conflict arises. Well Jesus knows the importance of confronting our brokenness. In fact he shows us a trick to dealing with our conflicts. He gives us a five-step resolution to conflict:

1. ***Discern the concern.*** *Decide if the issue will self-resolve or need intervention. If you take some time to reflect on the conflict, you may discover that you are part of the problem.*

2. **Make clean or intervene**. *If you still believe that you have been wronged, then you need to intervene. It's not going to be easy but try to work out the problem with just you and the other person.*

3. **Refer and confer**. *If the one-on-one intervention doesn't work, refer to others, presumably people without bias to fairly observe, and together confer.*

4. **Consult without insult**. *If the conferring intervention is of no success, take it to the larger community.*

5. **Act like Jesus**. *If nothing else works, then act like Jesus.*

So what's with step five? Step five brings us to the second mistake most people make when they read this text. Jesus continues, "and if the offender refuses to listen even to the church, let such a one be to you as a Gentile and a tax collector (v.17)." I have a study Bible that says Gentiles and tax collectors are to be treated as outsiders. [2] I have another, even harsher, study Bible that reads: "he or she is to be excluded from the fellowship and thought of as an unbeliever.[3]"

GENTILE

GENTILE MEANS NATION IN GREEK AND IS USED THROUGHOUT THE NEW TESTAMENT TO REFER TO ANY NON-JEW.

I recall once when I was attending a meeting of ministers and directors of religious groups. I was representing the mainline protestant ministries, but present also were Baptists, non-denominational folks, Muslims and Jews. As the meeting closed, one Christian minister stood up and said, "if all the believers could stay after, we need to do some real work." My heart sunk. That pastor used belief as a measure of exclusion.

---

[2] The Harper Collins Study Bible.
[3] ESV Study Bible.

That's why this minister and these study Bibles are wrong. Jesus wasn't excluding people as unbelievers or outsiders. Gentiles and tax collectors were very much part of Jesus' fellowship. We only have to flip a few pages back in Matthew and see that "as Jesus was walking along, he saw a man called Matthew sitting at a tax booth; and he said to him, 'Follow me.' And he got up and followed him (Matthew 9:9)." Did we just read, "tax booth"? The Scripture, in fact, teaches us that Jesus was a "friend" of sinners, tax collectors, gluttons, and drunks (See Matthew 11:19 or Luke 7:34). And so step five in Jesus' formula of resolution means only one thing: forgive them.[4] Don't exclude. Don't treat them as outsiders. Don't act as if you are the victor. Instead, forgive them.

> You know people who have seriously violated you or someone you love. This violation may have even been a serious crime. Let the thought of forgiving them rest on your heart. Try to capture this in words.

....

....

....

Forgiveness isn't something we are just called to do. It's not simply part of the Lord's Prayer to take up space. Forgiveness is part of God's nature and as people made in God's image we have it within us to offer forgiveness as well. When we forgive, even when its hard and even

---

[4] Of course some will disagree with this because in other places Jesus talks about seeking repentance in order to offer forgiveness (like Luke 17). I contend here, though, that step five trumps these occasions. Jesus' step five of forgiveness is the last option – which makes it the only option. Paul agrees when he writes "Bear with one another and, if anyone has a complaint against another, forgive each other; just as the Lord has forgiven you, so you also must forgive (Colossians 3:13)."

when we feel others may not be deserving, the power to forgive is liberating. The ability and power to forgive sets us apart.

> How else are we called to be set apart?

....

....

....

QUESTIONS

➤ Find two or three conflict resolution books in the library. There are tons. Check them out and thumb through them. Most have steps, charts, or even tables of contents that reveal their secrets. Have the group compare these formulas to Jesus' five steps.

➤ Divide the Bible into some smaller sections. From within each section, find how forgiveness is handled. For instance divide it like this: The Torah (first five books); History (Joshua to Esther); Wisdom (Job, Proverbs and even the book of Psalms); Prophets (Isaiah to Malachi); Gospels and the Book of Acts; and Letters (Romans and so forth).

CHAPTER 4

God's Guest List

SCRIPTURE

Read Romans 14

FIRST THINGS

Faith, at least for me, is always a roller coaster. Sometimes I am confident in my faith. Other times I show huge lapses in faith. In Romans 14, Paul urges the church to "welcome those who are weak in faith." It seems like I mess up with this simple task every time. Take for instance when I go to a night shelter to help the weak. When I arrive, I encounter someone who has been living on the streets, struggling every second, worried about where their next meal comes from but yet somehow is sharing a strong faith and welcoming me. Suddenly, I realize I'm the one with the weak faith.

Or when I travel on a mission trip, I go to help the weak. However, I seem to end up getting served in ways I could never imagine by those who I am supposed to serve. I'm always receiving more than I give. The weakness of my own faith is often exposed by the surprisingly strong faiths of others. Sometimes I wonder if Paul knew this would happen?

> Describe a time when the table was turned and you ended up receiving something when you were supposed to give.

STUDY

Romans 14 is an exceptional text, but Paul's style of writing can be difficult to follow. In circumstances like these, I find it helpful to take extra time with the text even if I have to rewrite it myself just to get the idea of what he's trying to say.

> Take some time and try to re-write Romans 14:1-12 in your own words:

_____

_____

_____

_____

_____

_____

_____

_____

_____

_____

_____

_____

_____

_____

_____

_____

When I re-wrote Romans 14 for myself, I gleaned a few points:
- ✓ *God welcomes everyone to the party. (v. 3)*
- ✓ *We ought not to change God's guest list. (v. 4)*
- ✓ *It's not our job to be the Christian police. (v. 5)*

- ✓ *All things should be done to honor God. (v. 6)*
- ✓ *If you and God are reconciled about an issue, don't worry what others think. (v. 7).*
- ✓ *We belong to God no matter what. (vs. 8 and 9)*
- ✓ *Judging others is a waste of our time. (v. 10)*
- ✓ *We're in God's hands. (vs. 11 and 12)*

Not changing God's guest list is a wild thought. It goes against our very nature. Anyone who has ever played dodgeball in school knows we would rather be the team captains. Captains pick their sides. And it's the power of a team captain that many of us desire. It may be selfish but as team captains we could choose the kids that were strong enough to take the lick for us. Dodgeball captains always pick mere pawns. Dodgeball teams, churches, classrooms, clubs, and workplaces often deal with power struggles. Statistically speaking, only a few can be team captains. Which means as long as there is power to be had, struggles for that power will follow. And the rest of us might just be pawns.

The history of humanity is soaked in power struggles. Consider Jean-Bertrand Aristide. After years of conflict and brutal regimes, Aristide, a priest in the world's poorest slums, rose to power and was elected president of Haiti. Within a year the Front for Democracy (a bloodthirsty opposition group) staged a coup and ousted the president.

Aristide's rise to power was fueled by his belief and engagement with liberation theology. Liberation theology presupposes that the Christian faith is to be seen, taught and lived through the eyes of poverty. Jesus liberated those who couldn't care for themselves. He spent most of his time with the poor and hungry. Jesus himself was poor. For the liberation theologian this was not accidental. Leonardo Boff writes:

Not only do the poor have needs that must be alleviated; they possess a singular wealth of their own. They are the chosen vessels of the Lord, the prime addressees of the Reign of God, the potential evangelizers of the Church and of the whole human race.[5]

One of my past professors used to teach that the Bible "comforts the afflicted and afflicts the comfortable." As opposed to a prosperity Gospel, Liberation theology thrives in the presence of the afflicted. Aristide chose to be prophetic within his community by preaching to the afflicted and against the afflicters. He followed the prophets of the Hebrew Bible, like Amos and Isaiah. I am sure Aristide probably quoted Jeremiah to the poorest of poor in the slums of Cite Soleil in Port-au-Prince saying "my voice will be heard everywhere on earth, accusing nations of their crimes and sentencing the guilty to death (Jeremiah 25:31, CEV)." After years of dictatorship, Aristide indeed captured the hearts of Haiti's poor. With persuasive rhetoric and the conviction of Liberation theology consider what Aristide himself says:

Do we hear God speaking through the poor? In a world oriented only toward profit, it may be difficult for us to hear God's voice above the din and the racket of the moneychangers who have filled the world's temples. But God is not the market. God is love. God is justice. God is peace.

God is also a woman. Wherever women are heard and respected, the face of God is illuminated. Wherever the poor are heard and respected, the face of God is illuminated. The gift of Christ is his humanity, his presence among the living, among the poor. Jesus is not only the God of glory; he is the God of suffering. He is quiet dignity in the face of misery, children

---

[5] Boff, Leonardo. Spirituality and Politics.

who still smile, mothers who give love even when there is no food, the
capacity to see hope through excruciating pain, acts of courage in the face
of violence, determination in the face of impunity.[6]

What Aristide says is very powerful, provocative, and true. I vividly recall a conversation I had with a former friend of Jean-Bertrand Aristide. I asked him how they met. As an Episcopal priest, he shared that Jean-Bertrand and him were close friends and worked together on many common causes. They shared similar beliefs and desires for the people of Haiti. He told me, however, that things changed. I'll never forget when he said "I used to know Jean-Bertrand," but I have never met "President Aristide." Sadly my friend was letting me know Aristide's power had become poisoned. Aristide's rise and fall in Haiti is well documented and my friend was right.

While liberation theology can be wonderful to some, it reminds me that whenever we're bent in any direction for too long we get weak on the other side. Some beliefs can wack our faith out of alignment. This applies as well to evangelical theology or fundamentalist theology. Whatever your leaning or whatever your belief, the Scripture forces us to balance life. In fact, we shouldn't ever force our own agenda on others and call it Christian. That is, we should never dominate the text, but instead we need to be intentional about letting the text dominate us.[7]

> What are your thoughts on Liberation Theology?

---

[6] Aristide, Jean-Bertrand. Eyes of the Heart: Seeking a path for the poor in the age of globalization.

[7] I have heard stories of pastors saying "I picked this Scripture because it fits my sermon," which is totally contrary to how we are supposed to approach the Scripture. We shouldn't ever look to the Bible to help support our already conceived notions.

....

....

....

Aristide rose and fell from power because his power was poisoned. Stanford professor Robert Sutton, and author of Good Boss, Bad Boss teaches that power poisons in three ways:

- ✓ *Once in power, even good people fall into the trap of becoming self-centered.*
- ✓ *As the powerful become self-centered, they loose sight of others and the reasons they became powerful.*
- ✓ *As the power strengthens, the powerful begin to think that the rules no longer apply to them.*

> Name an occasion when either you forced a religious agenda on someone or someone else forced his or her agenda on you?

....

....

....

QUESTIONS

➢ As a group list as many leaders as possible. Discuss their shared qualities. Among the list how many of these leaders have been power poisoned? Discuss how power affects leadership.

➢ Review the session individual questions. Ask for participants to share.

➤ Classical theologians often criticize liberation theology because they feel it reduces Jesus' divinity and marginalizes God's sovereignty. Have the group discuss what the sovereignty of God means.

➤ Review the common mission or task the group decided on and discuss its execution.

CHAPTER 5

Getting Sucker Punched

SCRIPTURE

Read Matthew 5:38-48

FIRST THINGS

There is a battle within the evangelical world.[8] The likes of Mark Driscoll and his neo-puritan friends are pitted against the likes of Brian McLaren and his emergent cohort. The battle has many fronts. The neo-puritans are known for their tough guy Jesus belief and the emergents would contend that Jesus was not such a tough guy after all. When it surfaced that Rob Bell was writing a book about heaven and hell, Driscoll and his friends countered even before they had a chance to read Bell's work.[9] Not long after, Francis Chan wrote an opposing book that accuses Bell and others of making up their faith.[10]

Really? Making up their own faith. Sucker punches are flying all around.

> Be honest, list some times when you've thrown the punches:

---

[8] I know … when is there not a battle among evangelicals or Christians in general for that matter?

[9] Asbury Seminary professor Ben Witherington blogged that he knew for certain that Harper was so tight with the release of Bell's book that Driscoll and his friends (like John Piper) wrote "farewell Rob Bell" before they even could read his book.

[10] Rob Bell's book is Love Wins: A Book About Heaven, Hell, and the Fate of Every Person Who Ever Lived. Francis Chan's book is Erasing Hell: What God said about eternity, and the things we made up.

> And, of course, you've been hit as well. List some of those:

STUDY

I recall learning the *lex talionis* in elementary school. This law of talion, or retribution, is an ancient principle used in many religions. We find the Hebrew Levitical law as follows:

> *Anyone who hits and kills a fellow human must be put to death. Anyone who kills someone's animal must make it good - a life for a life. Anyone who injures his neighbor will get back the same as he gave: fracture for fracture, eye for eye, tooth for tooth. What he did to hurt that person will be done to him. Anyone who hits and kills an animal must make it good, but whoever hits and kills a fellow human will be put to death (Leviticus 24:17-21, this law is also found in Exodus and Deuteronomy).*

Obviously from reading Matthew 5 Jesus was not only familiar with the law of retribution, but he also felt it needed reform. Perhaps eye for an eye wasn't working that well. It may have been a difficult law to manage effectively in the event that the wrong eye was poked out. Even if the law was executed with precision, its overt fairness raises red flags. Fairness, after all, is not a popular biblical concept. This law of retribution appears but a few verses before we learn of the Year of

Jubilee in Leviticus. Jubilee is certainly not fair. Jubilee is the every fifty year celebration where all debts are cancelled, all slaves are freed, and all land is returned to the rightful owners (Leviticus 25:8-17). And Jesus' new command to turn the other cheek … is not fair as well. In fact, Jesus' replacement is far from impartial.

> List some unfair circumstances that have been bugging you.

We all probably have a friend who is a conspiracist. This is your friend who comes up with the seemingly delirious explanation that someone isn't being fair, taking advantage of the situation and getting ahead through all the wrong ways. Regrettably, your friend may be right on some occasions, because we also have friends who are opportunistic and will help themselves when they can.

So when in Matthew 5 Jesus says, "you have heard that it was said," its Jesus' way of preparing us for conspiracy. We may live in a certain type of world, but to Jesus this world is in need of reform. You may be familiar with *this*, but Jesus wants *that*. Jesus is confronting the way we know the world and the way the crowds gathered around him knew their world. His crowds knew what eye for an eye meant, but the way of Jesus was different.

Michael Shermer offers the Baloney Detection Kit at Skeptic Magazine. Despite the fact that Shermer denies Bigfoot[11] and he still uses a typewriter, the Baloney Detection Kit can be very helpful. Maybe it can help you resolve the issues between Francis Chan and Rob Bell:

✓ *How reliable is the source?*

✓ *Does the source make similar claims?*

✓ *Have the claims been verified by someone else?*

✓ *Does this fit with the way the world works?*

✓ *Has anyone tried to disprove the claim?*

✓ *Where does the preponderance of evidence point?*

✓ *Is the claimant playing by the rules of science?*

✓ *Is the claimant providing positive evidence?*

✓ *Does the new theory account for as many phenomena as the old theory?*

✓ *Are personal beliefs driving the claim?*

In Matthew 5, Jesus is making a new claim. The old claim is eye for an eye. The new claim is turn your cheek. And Jesus lives the claim. He doesn't promise that we will never get sucker punched. In fact, quite the opposite exists. He invites it. Eye for eye and tooth for tooth don't fit into the way of the cross. And Jesus calls us to the cross. If anything is certain, taking up the cross is quite the opposite of taking an eye for an eye. In fact, not only are we supposed to take the punches one after another, we are called to punch back with shame. If you've ever been sucker punched the sting isn't the punch but rather the humiliation in throwing it. No one wants to be sucker punched for sure, but even worse is being blamed for throwing the sucker punch. It shows the cowardice of the offender. If someone sucker punches you, your biggest reward is his or

---

[11] I'm still holding onto the hope that I will one day find Bigfoot, Sasquatch, the Yeti, or the infamous Chupacabra.

her embarrassment. In other words, Jesus is saying that turning the cheek is not an act of non-resistance, but rather, it's an act of shaming and discrediting the violent.

And that's not fair.

> Give some examples of how Jesus flipped the situation.

....

....

....

The entire fifth chapter of Matthew, in fact, is saturated with these new claims of Jesus. Each is prefaced with Jesus saying, "you have heard it was said." We know what Jesus said about an eye for an eye. Here are the other four. Jesus says *you have heard it was said…*

- ✓ *Don't murder … but Jesus says don't even get angry.*
- ✓ *Don't sleep around … but Jesus says watch the way you lust.*
- ✓ *Be careful of what you promise … but Jesus says don't promise anything.*
- ✓ *Love your neighbor and hate your enemy … but Jesus says love both.*

As followers of Jesus we get sucker punched quite often, even by other Christians. *I have heard it was said* God hates gays and lesbians. But have you ever considered what Jesus really said? He doesn't even raise the issue. *I have heard it was said* that drinking alcohol is sinful. But Jesus drank wine. *I have heard it was said* that evolution theories are of the devil. But if God is as mighty as we sing, could not God create the world the way he desired? *I have heard it was said* that you must be baptized to receive salvation. But Jesus was baptized. Does that mean Jesus needed salvation? A task the Jesus follower has then, is to discern the sayings of the world, detect the baloney, and live to the claims of Jesus.

> Give some examples of things you have heard, but believe Jesus would disagree with.

....

....

....

QUESTIONS

➢ As a group watch Shermer's Baloney Detection Kit, found at Skeptic Magazine or YouTube.

➢ Review the session individual questions. Ask for participants to share.

➢ Thumb through the book of Leviticus. Share some of the laws and ancient codes you find. Make a list of laws you see as unfair and discuss their possible contexts.

➢ Review the common mission or task the group decided on and discuss its execution.

CHAPTER 6

Becoming Lost

SCRIPTURE

Read Luke 15:1-10

FIRST THINGS

Being lost occupies the minds of J.J. Abrams and other Hollywood Producers. If the setting isn't a remote Pacific island we can still be 'Lost in Translation'. We are also reminded of the fear of being lost when we enter a post office or drink from a milk carton. Phone poles across the city are scattered with flyers for lost dogs. We seem to have a knack for getting lost.

> When can you remembering be lost?

....

....

....

STUDY

While being lost is common it nonetheless remains perplexing. I recall when I was tasked to lead a group of college students to Lookout Point in the NC mountains. Although I wasn't confident in my ability to do so, I was the only one in the group who had been there. I had not only hiked to the point once, but actually I had blazed the trail multiple times. However, I had never been the leader. Regardless, we hiked ahead. The trail was easy to follow until after about a mile when it narrowed. Looking up, I felt I could see a ridge so we continued. The second mile we gained elevation fast and it wasn't easy. We did so until I could no longer see above me. We were at the top. However, we were not at Lookout Point. We were lost. But I was confused. I didn't feel as if I was getting lost. It really took me by surprise.

It's common sense that if we knew we were about to get lost we would at that point try to avoid it. But, of course, this rarely happens. Our minds trick us because we have this belief that we are right. And when we think we're right, we can't get lost. So, for instance, we set our keys down on a counter without contemplating the fact that we might just forget what we just did. And because we forget, we look everywhere ... but the counter. Likewise, on that hike, despite the fact that I had no recollection of where I had been I kept pressing ahead.

Former Intel CEO Andy Grove calls these tricky times 'strategic inflection points'.[12] He contends that in small ways we do know our keys will get lost. In the back of our mind, we do realize we can get lost on the mountain trail. We realize this, but yet ignore it. We don't get lost or fail or get defeated by accident, Grove argues. These things happen because we ignore the evidence. Leaders often fail not because of really bad decisions, but rather by ignoring the signposts. We get lost because we disregard where we've been, where we are, and where we're going. Gavin de Becker speaks of this in his book *The Gift of Fear* as well. He notes that victims of crime often discount their own sense of fear, intuition, or gut feelings.

---

[12] Grove, Andrew. Only the Paranoid Survive: How to Exploit the Crisis Points That Challenge Every Company.

> Point to some times that this has happened to you:

....

....

....

The people of Israel didn't wander in the wilderness for forty years because they were lost in the way a GPS system would understand. Their loss was in a form of a straggled resistance. They knew where they were but they just couldn't quite make it. A few years back I was in Arkansas just after a bad ice storm. Streets were closed and trees were down everywhere. As I was driving I knew where I was and I knew where I needed to go, but I just couldn't make it because of all the obstacles. I was lost in a straggled resistance.

> Share a time or two when you were lost in a straggled resistance.

....

....

....

In Luke 15 Jesus tells three parables. The first parable is about a lost sheep and the last parable is the story of the loving father. They are similar in that the characters strayed away and thus became lost. However, the middle parable is about a woman who looses her coin. As far as I can determine, I am pretty certain that the coin didn't wander off. I feel confident that it didn't get lost on its own. Which brings up something important: Being lost is not always our fault. And if the coin didn't realize that it was lost, equally so it would never know it was found. Regardless, God is like a woman who searches for what is lost. And God finds us, even if we remain unaware.

> God searches until he finds. God doesn't give up or give in. You were lost. Now you are found. How can you celebrate this?

....

....

....

QUESTIONS

➢ As a group watch one of the many short documentaries on YouTube featuring Gavin de Becker and discuss his theories on crime and victimization.

➢ Review the session individual questions. Ask for participants to share.

➢ Recently I lost a pair of glasses. When I looked in lost and found, I found a box of about 100 pairs. Think of some ways we can reduce waste and bring hope to others with all the items we lose and find.

CHAPTER 7

A Growing Heart

SCRIPTURE

Read Acts 11:19-30

FIRST THINGS

When my son was two-years old, doctors discovered a whole in his heart. Because his heart was working so hard, on a routine x-ray before his open-heart surgery, it was revealed that his heart was three times its normal size. We have a photo of him from about a month prior to his diagnoses. It was one of those black and white shots taken by the amusement park on a kiddie rollercoaster ride. Every time we look at the picture, we laugh at Dr. Seuss' books and say "Caleb's heart grew three sizes that day."

> Name some serious occasions in your life that can be interpreted with humor by books or movies.

....

....

....

STUDY

The Book of Acts is the church's first piece of history. Acts is the *Two Tower's* to Luke's *Fellowship of the Ring*. In other words, Acts is a sequel that didn't tank. As a saga Luke and Acts have shared themes and one prominent theme is that of belongings – those tangible things in life we have. The books challenge our views of property, possessions, and money:

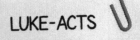

LUKE-ACTS

BOTH LUKE AND ACTS ARE ANONYMOUS WORKS. PEOPLE SOMETIMES THINK LUKE THE PHYSICIAN WROTE THEM, BUT THERE IS NO SUCH EVIDENCE. SCHOLARS DO THINK, THOUGH, THE TWO BOOKS WERE WRITTEN BY THE SAME PERSON.

- ✓ *Share your coats (Luke 3:11)*
- ✓ *Give to beggars (Luke 6:30)*
- ✓ *Give alms (Luke 11:41)*
- ✓ *Sell your possessions (Luke 12:32, 18:22)*
- ✓ *Share everything (Acts 2:44, 4:32)*

> Name some ways to improve the way you share.

....

....

....

Charitable practice in the days of Jesus, however, had become a platform for self-affirmation. The elite and wealthy would "give alms" as a way to promote themselves and their agenda.[13] So Jesus felt almsgiving needed reframing. He questioned how people prayed and fasted. He reframed how people treated one another and how we share. The act of giving itself is good, but Jesus was clear that self-promotion should never be a motivating factor for anything, especially service. The prophet Isaiah challenged this sort of volunteerism as well:

---

[13] Matthew 6:2 notes, The New Interpreter's Study Bible.

Do you think this is the kind of fast day I'm after: a day to show off humility? To put on a pious long face and parade around solemnly in black? Do you call that fasting, a fast day that I, God, would like? "This is the kind of fast day I'm after: to break the chains of injustice, get rid of exploitation in the workplace, free the oppressed, cancel debts. What I'm interested in seeing you do is: sharing your food with the hungry, inviting the homeless poor into your homes, putting clothes on the shivering ill-clad, being available to your own families (Isaiah 58:5-7, THE MESSAGE).

Intent is huge. Jesus and Isaiah are saying something like: '*so what ... you give to the poor. Big deal.*' The shared message of Jesus and Isaiah wasn't concerned with giving away possessions. The community in Acts wasn't asked to part with their stuff. Spring cleanings and trips to the Goodwill weren't the intent. Instead, the first disciples were asked to provide. There's a difference between giving over money and sharing your wealth. There's a difference between dropping off a can of food and opening up your table for dinner. The former implies that an exchange has been made, its market driven, and the transaction is over. The latter suggests that this act of giving is the beginning of a relationship.

If we don't avoid the book altogether, sometimes we get caught up in all of the laws found in Leviticus. To be sure, many of the Levitical laws are extreme. But what if the intent of the law wasn't oppression but instead progression? Could have all of the laws been a means to progress Israel? Biblical scholar John Dominic Crossan suggests that we read the fine print in every contract. And the Torah is no exception. Getting beyond the tiresome laws and codes, we can find some very relevant concerns, such as:

✓ *Forbidding Interest*

✓ *Freeing Slaves*

✓ *Controlling Collateral*

✓ *Remitting Debts*

✓ *And Reversing Dispossession*[14]

Forbidding interest and freeing slaves are very progressive laws that are very relevant today. What would the world be like if we forbid interest? Imagine the lives of those stuck with credit card debt if we used Biblical law to guide the way we share our resources? And consider the pervasiveness of human trafficking. In 2009 Oakland's Child Exploitation Unit made 640 arrests offering kids money for sex.[15]

> Give a modern example of controlling collateral:

....

....

....

> Give a modern example of remitting debts:

....

....

....

---

[14] Crossan, John Dominic. God & Empire: Jesus against Rome, then and now.

[15] Flynn, Mary. As more Oakland youth join the sex trade, law enforcement explores alternatives to incarceration.

> Give a modern example of reversing dispossession:

....

....

....

About ten years ago, one of my mentors in ministry took me to lunch. On the way to the restaurant we stopped by a large church and he asked me to come inside. I figured he needed to pick up a package or leave a message, so I didn't think much of it. So when we arrived at the church office I was pretty startled when he said, "my friend here (referring to me) needs a Bible." With an intensity that could make me cry he continued, "do you have one to spare?" The secretary quickly replied "no." They went back and forth a few times, but she won and we left for the car without a Bible. I didn't really need a Bible so I wasn't all that upset. But my mentor certainly had me thinking about how churches sometimes can treat outsiders. Inside I was thanking him for the lesson.

Then we arrived at the diner. Before I knew it he was up to it again. But instead of the church secretary, he asked the hostess. A few minutes later our waitress brought a Bible and some cash. It seemed word got out and the staff asked their customers if anyone had a Bible. Sure enough someone was willing to give one away and even though we didn't ask for any money a few dollars arrived as well. After lunch, we passed the Bible and cash on to someone else.

I still think about that lesson of compassion quite often. My mentor taught me the difference between giving alms and having a big heart. You would think that giving a Bible away isn't such a big deal, for either the church or a stranger at a diner. After all, I can buy a box of fifty

Bibles for about $30. We did this once on our way to Mexico. The all-Spanish versions may have been even cheaper. So one afternoon in a small Mexican village we decided to spread some cheer in a way to honor my mentor and start giving Bibles away like the Gideons do on campuses and at hotels. It was only $30 worth, so what could we lose? But as the box of fifty dwindled, one student named Nick had an amazing encounter with a wrinkled and feeble lady in her mid nineties. As she grabbed tightly to the Bible she said to Nick *"he estado esperando toda mi vida para este,"* or "I've been waiting all my life for this."

> Make a list of times you have showed compassion. Then evaluate the intent of these actions.

....

....

....

QUESTIONS

➤ Discuss what your group can do with a box of Bibles. Maybe you have a great idea of how to make a lasting impact.

➤ Read 2 Corinthians 9:7. Discuss the importance of intentional giving and resourcefulness.

CHAPTER 8

Blessed Poverty

SCRIPTURE

Read Luke 12:32-37

FIRST THINGS

You may be familiar with the friar St. Francis of Assisi, founder of the Franciscan Order. Many including a young girl named Clare, admired the work of St. Francis. Clare, in fact, turned away her family's wealth to follow Francis' understanding of the Gospel. Although Clare had to escape her inheritance and privileged life, she did so in a way that convinced her mother, sister and aunt to eventually do the same.

> Can you imagine escaping from a life of wealth? Is there something in your life that the world admires but your gut tells you to leave behind?

STUDY

Some people are convinced that beggars are those who can't sober themselves up for the urban rescue centers, so therefore you see them on the corners. I know others who argue that street begging is very profitable. [16] Some cities (like Nashville and Durham) have their 'traditional' beggars sell newspapers instead. And in some places (like Long Beach) street begging is a crime. However, Clare of Assisi is the first person I have ever heard of who purposefully gave her life over to begging. Clare chose to beg as a sign of unity with the poor.

> Clare was a street beggar. What would you think of someone – what would you tell your friends about someone – who intentionally gave up wealth to street beg out of an act of solidarity with the poor?

....

....

....

> I have a hard time distinguishing between street begging and what non-profit executives do. How do you define begging and how does it differ from fundraising?

....

....

....

....

Study after study show that people believe if only they earned a higher income, happiness would follow. Contrast this to Clare's letter to her friend and contemporary Agnes of Prague.[17] Clare wrote about her new life of poverty:

---

[16] I doubt this, and it sounds like another elitist way to ignore poverty.
[17] Agnes was canonized by Pope John Paul II on November 12, 1989

O blessed poverty,
who bestows eternal riches
on those who love and embrace her!

O holy poverty,
to those who possess and desire you
God promises the kingdom of heaven and offers,
indeed, eternal glory and blessed life!

O God-centered poverty,
whom the Lord Jesus Christ who ruled
and now rules heaven and earth,
who spoke and things were made,
condescended to embrace before all else![18]

> Blessed, holy, God-centered poverty? What are your thoughts?

....

....

....

Admittedly, thousands of people have lived a full life to God expressed in a devotion to the poor and outcast. We may be able to think of the Mother Teresas and the Dorothy Days of the world. Service to and with the poor is also done effectively outside the Christian community. So while service to the poor is certainly a mark of following Christ, it is also a virtue that is not exclusively Christian.

---

[18] Clare of Assisi. Excerpt from Mueller.

Clare's motivation, however, was uniquely Christian. She writes "I am sure that the kingdom of heaven is promised and given by the Lord only to the poor."[19]

God's kingdom given only to the poor?

Traditionally we tend to think of the kingdom of heaven as up high and Earth as down here. I have heard preachers talk about how Jesus leaves his plush kingdom and enters the grungy Earth. And even the Nicene Creed states that Jesus "for us and for our salvation … came down from heaven." For Clare, however, the kingdom of heaven is never that far away. In fact, Jesus repeatedly calls people to "repent, for the kingdom of heaven is near (Matthew 4:17)." Other translations render the same verses "repent, for the kingdom of heaven is at hand." [20]

The Greek word used in Matthew 4:17 is *eggizō*, which means both near and at hand. The kingdom of heaven is both near and at hand and this is a reality that Clare new. Jesus didn't leave the kingdom of heaven to come to Earth but rather brought his kingdom with him. When Clare says God's kingdom is given only to the poor she is stating an awareness to reality more so than a belief. For Clare, service is eschatological. In other words, Clare felt service to the poor was related to the end times; in order to realize Jesus' return, today we need to serve the poor. The world for her – which is also the world for us – is the same world that Jesus interrupted. More so, Clare saw her role as helping to usher the new kingdom with Jesus' return.

---

[19] Clare of Assisi, Excerpt from Mueller.
[20] Among those are the New American Standard Version and the King James Bible.

> N.T. Wright, the Bishop of Durham England, writes, "God's kingdom is happening under your noses, and you can't see it." [21] I believe Clare would agree. Would you? Take some time to reflect on this:

....

....

....

QUESTIONS

➢ For Clare, service was uniquely Christian. How do you distinguish between Christian service and everyday philanthropy?

➢ Review the session individual questions. Ask for participants to share.

➢ Often street beggars perform with their music or art. Discuss as a group your thoughts about begging, street performance, and its alternatives.

➢ Review the common mission or task the group decided on and discuss its execution.

---

[21] Wright, N.T. Simply Christian: Why Christianity makes sense.

CHAPTER 9

Leaving a Legacy

SCRIPTURE

Read Exodus 3:1-8

FIRST THINGS

When Yahweh first promised Moses in Exodus 3 that he would deliver the people of Israel and give them a land flowing with milk and honey, God did so with a cost. This land was occupied by others ... the Canaanites, Hittites, Amorites and so forth. Confrontation was ingrained in such a promise. Strings were attached.

> What promises have you made that had strings attached, both intended and unintended?

YAHWEH

YAHWEH IS THE NAME USED FOR LORD IN THE HEBREW BIBLE. IT WAS USED MORE THAN 6,000 TIMES. THE HEBREW WORD FOR GOD, ELOHIM, WAS USED LESS THAN HALF AS MANY TIMES.

STUDY

If you grew up sheltered in a way that prevented you from experiencing bad stuff, you may have been indoctrinated with what Dallas Willard calls the "gospel of sin management."[22] The training begins innocuously as a method to block kids from music and movies with suggestive lyrics. Thus a family may play only the Christian radio station. As the child becomes older, parents increase the levels of prevention from media to restricting certain types of relationships and friends. Eventually, some kids are pulled from public school or deeply encouraged to attend a Christian college. The underlying intent is to avoid sin and as Willis contends this method of sin management starts to embed itself in our lives as a core value of following Jesus.

Alternatively, some Amish often observe a time called Rumspringa, when sixteen year-olds experience the "world of the English." Tom Shachtman's book Rumspringa: To Be or Not To Be Amish sheds light on this interesting phase of life. According to Shachtman, Rumspringa is the counter-narrative to the gospel of sin management. In this rite of passage many Amish experience wild parties, lots of drugs and sex. In contrast to the gospel of sin management, parents hope these young Amish would grow and discover the beauty and wisdom of their church amidst the brokenness of the world.

Like most of the rest of us, having no gospel of sin management nor Rumspringa, Mary McLeod Bethune was conditioned by her time. Growing up in South Carolina as a poor girl in the late 1800s to parents who had been slaves, Mary witnessed firsthand the brutal grip of oppression and the determination to see change. She couldn't manage the sin around her. But, instinctively she knew how the world worked wasn't right. Post Civil War times in the south gave rise to the KKK, lynchings, 'black codes,' and all types of violence and segregation.

---

[22] I first heard this phrase from Kara Powell and Chap Clark's book Sticky Faith: Everyday ideas to build lasting faith in your kids.

Unlike the gospel of sin management, and more like the life of Jesus, she had no choice but to face the sin that surrounded her.

And Mary did not let the conditions of the time dictate a place for her in the world. Instead, Mary was motivated by a hope in God's call. Recognizing that she was a child of God, she knew she had it within her to rise above the oppression of the south. She started this inward journey by trying to learn as much as she could.

Mary simply, but profoundly, recognized the power of knowledge. As her inward journey unfolded she knew that it was God's will to extend her call to others, so she started to teach. Quickly Mary started her own school for African American girls and within a few years she created what is known today as Bethune-Cookman University in Daytona Beach.

> List some of your own inward journey discoveries and ways that you can extend them beyond yourself to others.

....

....

....

Mary McLeod Bethune lived a commissioned life. Consider the number of commissioning stories in the Bible. Notably, Yahweh assured Moses, in his commissioning that he had seen, heard, and knew of the suffering of his people. It's striking how their commissions parallel:

✓ *Yahweh appears to Moses in a burning bush, and calls him to a life of service (Exodus 3). God appears to Mary in a burning post-war south and calls her into a life of service.*

56

- ✓ *God equips Moses with strengths and abilities (Exodus 4). God equips Mary with the opportunity for an education and a determination to pass it on.*
- ✓ *Moses journeys out of Egypt on a mission. Mary, likewise, begins her mission in the wilderness.*

> How has God called you? What gifts has God given you to start this legacy of faith?

....

....

....

Leaving a legacy isn't something only for the wealthy. Once we move our inward calls to external calls we begin to leave legacies that are beneficial to the world. Consider the richness of Mary's legacy:

- ✓ *I leave you love.*
- ✓ *I leave you hope.*
- ✓ *I leave you a thirst for education.*
- ✓ *I leave you faith.*
- ✓ *I leave you racial dignity.*
- ✓ *I leave you a desire to live harmoniously.*
- ✓ *I leave you finally a responsibility to our young people.* [23]

> Mary's legacy wasn't simply articulated in a series of statements, but in the life she lived. She wrote, "the Freedom Gates are half-a-jar. We must pry them fully open." What do you strive to leave a future generation:

---

[23] Bethune, Mary McLeod. You can access her entire Last Will and Testament at http://www.cookman.edu/about_BCU/history/lastwill_testament.html

....

....

....

QUESTIONS

➤ As a group develop your own last will and testament.

➤ Review the session individual questions. Ask for participants to share.

➤ Discuss the gospel of sin management and the Amish rite of passage Rumspringa.

➤ Review the common mission or task the group decided on and discuss its execution.

CHAPTER 10

The Forty-Day Challenge

SCRIPTURE

Read Luke 4:1-13

FIRST THINGS

You might have the nicest BMW or Hummer available, but if you run out of gas – oh well. You may have a beautiful Hobie Cat, but if you have no wind for the sail – forget it. You may have purchased the best Giant or Trek bike on the market, but if your legs are broken – never mind.

> We have times when we feel empty. We can feel stuck or in a rut, or just burned out. Name some of those feelings you get:

....

....

....

STUDY

Morgan Spurlock, the brains behind "Super Size Me," also created "30 Days," a documentary series that lasted a few years on the FX network. The idea was that if you spend 30 days in a situation different than what you are used to, you would gain a greater appreciation and awareness of the world. We see TV shows, in particular, crop up like this continually. "Same Name" is a show where a famous person switches lives with someone of his or her same name. "Wife Swap," does the same but with wives. The series "Undercover Boss" would disguise a company's CEO, as he or she would go undercover into the daily operations of the business to experience both the good and bad of their companies. While these shows rarely survive a second season, the concept remains sticky.

A recent example of this comes from former Moral Majority executive and Liberty University dean Ed Dobson who wrote *The Year of Living Like Jesus*.[24] The book carries the reader through each month of Dobson's life "trying to eat, pray, talk and even vote as Jesus would. His revelation: Being Jesus is tough." [25] Think about it:

> *His initial commitment to keep kosher, observe Jewish holy days, not shave and read the four gospels weekly expands into an exploration of Judeo-Christian devotional practices. Seeking teachers from several religious traditions, Dobson incorporates Jewish prayers, the Catholic rosary, Orthodox prayer rope and Episcopal prayer beads into his daily devotional life. The book's form morphs from a somewhat choppy daily log into a series of thoughtful reflections on traditions he engages and gospel stories whose messages Dobson aspires to live. Weaving in tales of his fundamentalist roots, work with Jerry Falwell and long-term pastorate, Dobson reflects on the evolution of his religious consciousness: while maintaining a devout prolife stand, he votes for Barack Obama. With dignity and humor, the author addresses his personal struggle with ALS, seeking to model a prayerful response to his degenerative illness on Jesus' approach to suffering and healing. Dobson's strong faith, open mind,*

---

[24] After having a change of view and leaving Liberty University and the Moral Majority, Dobson pastored Calvary Church in Grand Rapids, which launched Rob Bell's pastorate at Mars Hills Church. Dobson retired from Calvary after being diagnosed with Lou Gehrig's disease.

[25] Honey, Charles. Could you live like Jesus for a year? This pastored tried.

humility (I'm a confused individual!) and compassion infuse this offering
from a self-proclaimed follower of Jesus.[26]

> What do you think about these self-motivated challenges?

....

....

....

People like SMU Professor Elaine Heath, Jonathan Wilson-Hartgrove, Donald Miller, Shane Claiborne and Alan Hirsch have popularized the new monastic movement. Unlike traditional monasticism, which entails a strict discipline toward a particular rule of life, new monastic movements are less regulated and depend more on covenants and community. Committing to some form of study, prayer, and service members of newer monastic communities still devote most of their lives toward a shared Christian journey. For many a new monastic life is similar to what Ed Dobson tried to recreate for himself.

Setting aside a year or more to live more radically for Jesus in the way of Ed Dobson or Jonathan Wilson-Hartgrove seems unreasonable for most. While I certainly admire their faith and mostly envy their practice of the gospel, I struggle to justify the fact I own a Chevy Tahoe, shop at Target and am very much part of the power grid. That is to say, I often struggle with my own footprint against the simplistic nature of the gospel. So if you're like me, a non-monastic, we have basically two choices. We can either suffer from gospel paralysis or we can be like Bill Murray and

---

[26] Publishers Weekly. August 2009.

make baby steps.[27] Gospel paralysis is our inability to change or transform. Basically getting stuck because we're on empty. Baby steps, however would be our ability to make small moves toward a greater goal, like Spurlock's 30 days.

Google engineer and blogger Matt Cutts also takes the 30-day challenge every so often and discovers some helpful life changes. Some of his personal challenges are soft, like deciding to bike to work everyday. While other challenges were difficult, like his hike up Kilimanjaro. Yet, both the easy and more difficult challenges taught him equally:

✓   *His life became more meaningful and vivid.*
✓   *His self-confidence grew.*
✓   *His small changes actually became sustainable.* [28]

> Make a list of some new things you can do for a period of 30 days:

....

....

....

Jesus' time in the wilderness, where the Synoptics record him being for forty days, was a great example of self-discipline. Here Jesus is led by the Spirit away from human structures. Here, "supernatural forces moved unfettered." [29] What Jesus experienced in the wilderness foreshadowed

---

[27] Baby Steps – From the movie What About Bob.
[28] I gleaned this info on Cutts from his TED speech: Try something new for 30 days.
[29] Foster, Richard. A Year with God: Living Out the Spiritual Disciplines.

what he faced in his life and at the cross. And for the reader, his 40-day challenge helps us grasp the larger message.

Temptation and sin get between God and us. But so can laziness, apathy and depression. It's as if they crowd the middle seat of a plane between you and the one you love. And they are fat! And its not like you can just kick the person out of his or her seat. Similarly, Jesus didn't stop the temptation while he was in the wilderness. Rather, he confronted it.

> What are some issues in your own life that you need to confront?

....

....

....

QUESTIONS

➤ Develop a list of possible 30 or 40-day challenges.

➤ Review the session individual questions. Ask for participants to share.

➤ Ed Dobson's journey to live like Jesus

➤ Study up on the new monastic movement. Either watch a short documentary on YouTube about a particular community or plan to visit one as a group.

CHAPTER 11

When Everything Goes Wrong

SCRIPTURE

Read Zephaniah 1:12-18

FIRST THINGS

Let's just get the record straight. God doesn't cause disaster. Pat Robertson and the 700 Club assertions that God's wrath caused Hurricane Katrina or that Haiti is cursed, is just bad theology.

> What are some examples of bad theology that you have come across?

....

....

....

STUDY

Bad theology is a way of describing a system of beliefs that doesn't jive with the Biblical narrative. We see the bulk of bad theology when people use the Bible out of context. While this is entirely subjective I contend that bad theology is rarely a misinterpretation of Scripture. It's not like the words Hurricane and Katrina are in the Scripture. So suggesting that God cursed New Orleans with a hurricane is very presumptuous. More often than not, assumptions (and thus bad theologies) are driven by specific agenda. Perhaps, in the case of television ministries the agenda is profit. Just Google TV evangelist scandals.

But most of us do not know TV preachers or rich Christian authors who make a living off of fear. So typically when we hear bad theology it's not because of Scriptural misinterpretation but rather a case of following the wrong crowd. Every once in awhile I hear someone say something like "God wanted me stuck in traffic to teach me patience." Or "God needed my sister in heaven more than me." When someone tells us (or when we believe ourselves) God caused *this* and God caused *that* ... be cautious. Applying caution is necessary because often such a belief aligns better with a particular personal assumption than anything found in the Scriptures. God didn't curse Haiti. God didn't send Katrina to destroy New Orleans. Sometimes the birds just strike.

> The book of Job never gives an answer to "why do bad things happen," but it asks the question over and over. In a prayerful way, list your suffering questions to God:

On January 15, 2009 the engines of US Airways Flight 1549 struck Canadian Geese. It was just after takeoff in the sky above New York City. Within six minutes the huge Airbus was in the Hudson River. I have the fortune of knowing a flight 1549 survivor. He happened to be the last passenger off the plane. His experience is remarkable. After all, how many people live to speak about their plane crash? After conducting cabin sweeps in the flooded plane making sure every passenger was safe, Dave was forced to jump into the icy river and swim to a rescue boat. In fact, he was one of the few passengers hospitalized.

Everyone survived flight 1549 and thus its easy for us to identify the story as miraculous. The media even named it the "Miracle on the Hudson." Despite this miracle, many of the passengers still struggle with the crash. Some of these cases are very serious and troublesome. They might contend that if a miracle really happened the birds would have never struck. We also talk a lot about miracles in more tragic situations. We hear of miracle stories near the Twin Towers on 9/11, for example. Family members of survivors will speak of how God's hand protected their father or sister. Perhaps their belief is spot on. However, it's more difficult to explain the miracle of God's intervention to family members of those who died. Which is it? Does God intervene for some and not for others? Was God present to rescue just a few?

I don't believe God sent those birds into the plane's engine. Likewise, I don't think God sent the pilots into the birds. But I do affirm Dave's faith when he says, "God wanted me there to help people and to do the right thing." It's hard to really get what Dave is saying. He's a plane crash survivor. I'm not. Actually I can't even imagine this. Yet he believes God wanted him there.

The trauma of flight 1549 reminds us that in seconds our life can change. Seconds! Just consider how quick the planes went into the towers. Or how quick a car crashes. Bad things are right around the corner. So we can ask God all we want to prevent the bad, but we just may have to realize God doesn't work in that way. God's given us the ability to prevent and prepare for bad things. And when we fail to do so (because we will), then we can ask God to equip us to bounce back and do what is right.

As a plane crash survivor, Dave offers an incredible bank of wisdom and helps me to reconcile for myself the tragedies I have faced. His reaction to help and respond to those in need was almost innate. His story is heroic in the sense that he really persuades me to prepare to do the same.

> Dave remained calm and responded immediately as a helper. How do you think you would have acted in this moment?

....

....

....

The amazing, perhaps miraculous, part of the story to me is how Dave continues to help. His actions and reactions are filled with wisdom and value. What Dave did on the Hudson continues to leverage critical response today in situations apart from what would be considered breaking news, like:

✓ *Spending time with family and friends. Dave has taught me relationships always trump tasks and projects.*

✓ *Seeing death. Dave has taught me that those who face death can also see the future and realize second chances.*

✓ *Giving thanks. Dave has taught me that we can't possibly thank God enough for what we already have.*

✓ *Recognizing the smaller miracles. Dave received a miracle on the Hudson for sure. And Dave continues to recognize countless other miracles, like having food on the table, having a job, and seeing the stars at night. Just sharing his story to thousands, Dave has experienced miracle after miracle after miracle.*

✓ *Attending to the distractions. Dave has taught me that those distractions that annoy us may be messages for us to attend to something more important.*

✓ *Listening is priceless. Dave taught me that we all think we have everything under control. For example, who pays attention to the flight attendants? Well, now Dave does for sure.*

> What are some things survivors have taught you?

....

....

....

QUESTIONS

> Zephaniah is a rather scary text, as God searches the city with lanterns in search for those deserving punishment. What do you make of this prophet's bleakness?

> Find a Bible tract and have the group discern its theological position. If you have multiple tracts that are different, read a few pages and then have the group anticipate its outcome. Or try determining if you can extricate the tract's theology from the Bible itself.

> Review the common mission or task the group decided on and discuss its execution.

CHAPTER 12

Dark Nights of the Soul

SCRIPTURE

Read Matthew 27:45-46

FIRST THINGS

In her diaries, Mother Teresa, shared her personal convictions. She wrote "In my own soul, I feel the terrible pain of this loss. I feel that God does not want me, that God is not God and that he does not really exist."

> What do you make of Mother Teresa's words?

STUDY

Mother Teresa felt called to work with the poorest of the poor. Every minute of every day she saw the reality of abuse, neglect, hunger, sickness and death. Imagine being within the walls of her Calcutta Missionaries for Charity. Conditions would be tight. Smells and noises would be intense and from wall to wall you would see rows upon rows of people suffering in small, yet adequate, cots. Some would have HIV, others would have tuberculosis and still others would be in misery suffering from any sort of deadly viruses. Many would be deteriorating from cancer, while others would be languishing in agony from accidents and injury.

Now, imagine seeing this every day. Every single day.

Still, we complain when we get a paper cut, when it rains, and when traffic is jammed. We'll complain about anything.

Although I have experienced tragedy in my own life, it seems each time I can pull away and at least experience a beautiful sunset. It seems that no matter what happens, I can at least escape for a minute and watch people laugh. No matter what has happened in my life, I have always been able to realize I'm not alone. Even when I feel alone, I know others have felt similarly. So far, I've been super lucky.

Yet, it's probably safe to assume Mother Teresa never allowed for much self-reflection time. Her life was consumed with others. And almost always those others were in significant pain. In fact, it is rare to find a picture of her smiling. It's likely that she was thinking about the hardship of others. Her loved poured out so much that she truly emptied herself of everything – even her own comfort in God.

> What if truly following Jesus meant denying yourself (Mark 8:34) of all personal gain – even comfort, hope and feeling loved by God?

The Scripture is certainly challenging. Its demand that we take up the cross and follow Jesus (Luke 9:23) is far from some poetic verse to throw around. And I suppose if we are true to the Scripture it can leave us feeling pretty guilty as we continue to shop and hoard, waste food, drive our SUVs, worry, and fall short. In fact, we always fall short of living right "by what we have done, and by what we have left undone."[30]

Then again most of us live in some sort of guilt no matter what path we follow. Guilt can really do a number on us for sure. There are just those times in life when we are tired and worn down. Sometimes our thoughts exhaust us and leave us empty. Oddly enough, we may feel an absence from God when we throw ourselves on the frontline and see the hurt in others. And we even may feel God has abandoned us when times are going well. Guilt haunts these times as well.

Early Christian mystics, however, did not call these feelings guilt. Rather, they called these feelings the Dark Night. Sixteenth Century mystic St. John of the Cross wrote a poem called Dark Night of the Soul. And, consider what John's Gospel teaches us about this dark night:

✓ *The light shines in the darkness, and the darkness did not overcome it. (John 1:5)*

✓ *And this is the judgment, that the light has come into the world, and people loved darkness rather than light because their deeds were evil. (John 3:19)*

✓ *Again Jesus spoke to them, saying, 'I am the light of the world. Whoever follows me will never walk in darkness but will have the light of life.' (John 8:12)*

---

[30] From the Confession of Sin, Rite II, Book of Common Prayer.

✓ *Jesus said to them, 'The light is with you for a little longer. Walk while you have the light, so that the darkness may not overtake you. If you walk in the darkness, you do not know where you are going.' (John 12:35)*

✓ *I have come as light into the world, so that everyone who believes in me should not remain in the darkness. (John 12:46)*

Especially when I'm at the beach, I'm reminded of how dark dark is. The darkness of night covers a path and makes it hard to follow. Sometimes you can't even see two feet in front of you. However, the next morning when you walk the same path (that has only been exposed by the light of the sun) it's a cakewalk. It's like the path was dramatically changed. But, of course, the path never changed.

The Hebrew Bible begins by painting the picture of the earth as welter and waste[31] ... a sense of complete darkness awaiting illumination. And, the Scripture doesn't teach us that darkness is evil. Darkness isn't a great dualistic warrior with light. John's Gospel clearly exemplifies this. On the contrary, Scripture teaches us that darkness simply describes something yet to be exposed. What isn't illuminated is harder to see. So Jesus describes himself as a light helping to illuminate the dark nights of our soul.

> Sometimes we can find comfort in Jesus' light. Other times it's more difficult. We read in the Psalms that the word is a 'lamp' and we are

---

[31] I believe Robert Alter's translation of "welter and waste" is probably the best rendering of the Hebrew from Genesis 1:2. Consider these different translations: NRSV - formless void; NIV - formless and empty; King James – Without form and void; Common English Bible - without shape or form. Alter's translation helps to explain perhaps a more accurate understanding of what existed before creation. By welter and waste he is contending that the Genesis narrative is trying to explain why God created the earth, not how or from what.

also called to be the 'light of the world.' List some people or experiences that have illuminated your life:

....

....

....

QUESTIONS

➢ Ask for prayer requests and open with prayer.

➢ Open with prayer.

➢ Read the text: Matthew 27:45-46

➢ Discuss what theologian Peter Rollins means when he says "the only church that illuminates is a burning one," in what he has coined pyro-theology.

➢ Review the session individual questions. Ask for participants to share.

➢ Break into two smaller groups. Have one group consider all the times the Bible refers to darkness and the other light. Then have the groups dual their positions. Was anything learned?

CHAPTER 13

Preparing for the Journey

SCRIPTURE

Read Mark 1:1-3

FIRST THINGS

The Christian calendar begins with Advent, the season that anticipates the incarnation of Jesus Christ. As Mary waited with Jesus in her womb, so Israel waited hundreds of years like an expectant mother for the Messiah. They both waited for incarnation, God's breakthrough into the world we live. But Advent is more than just waiting. Advent is like college: A season to prepare.

INCARNATION

INCARNATION MEANS TO BECOME FLESH AND REPRESENTS THE EMBODIMENT OF GOD IN THE PERSON JESUS OF NAZARETH. TO LIVE INCARNATIONALLY WOULD THEN MEAN TO EMBODY JESUS IN OUR OWN LIVES.

> Students prepare for college and brides and grooms prepare for weddings. How do you prepare for God's coming?

....

....

....

STUDY

When my dad was in high school he didn't take any AP classes to prepare for college. He didn't study for the SAT or ACT. Standardized tests and concerns for his academic record weren't existent. And I am fairly certain his school didn't have any counselors or college prep advisors. So when my Grandpop called the dean at the University of North Carolina to enroll my dad, it wasn't a big deal. That fall he started taking classes as a Tarheel. Dad was a good student, but imagine getting into any school, let alone a top tier college, with no application.

My dad's experience is hard for me to grasp as today elementary students face standardized tests, have advanced classes like AIG and students as early as kindergarten are studying foreign language emersion. My second grader takes both Chinese and Spanish ... and she's in public school.

Historically it was common for Jewish children to memorize the Torah. It is safe to assume that most contemporaries of Jesus and Jesus himself memorized parts of or even the entire Hebrew Bible. They were well studied in rabbinical writings, moral codes, midrash and even the classics. The early Christian church continued this rigorous education through Catechesis, a formal program of study.

Are you familiar with catechesis?

Today, the phrase Christian Education seems to be an oxymoron. Christian confirmation is typically a time where sixth graders make popsicle stick Jesus figures. In fact, serious Christian education is sparse. "According to recent polls, most American adults cannot name even one of the four Gospels, and many high-school seniors think that Sodom and Gomorrah were husband and wife." [32]

---

[32] Prothero, Stephen. Religious Literacy: What Every American Needs to Know--And Doesn't.

> Boston University professor Stephen Prothero, who is quoted just above, has a biblical literacy test in the back of his book. How would you fair with some of his questions:

✓ *"God helps those who help themselves." Is this in the Bible? If so, where?*
✓ *What are the first five books of the Hebrew Bible?*
✓ *Name the Ten Commandments.*
✓ *What is the Golden Rule?*

The Gospel of Mark begins with a declaration by John the Baptist, citing the prophet Isaiah saying "Prepare the way of the Lord, make his paths straight (Mark 1:3)." This quote from Isaiah 40 refers to a highway being prepared for the Jews to use to return home from exile. During the exodus, Israel fled Egypt's oppression and rule. During the exile the Jews faced Babylon's brutality and prayed for a day to return to their Promised Land much like their ancestors before.

Could John the Baptist, who's calling his followers to prepare the way of the Lord, be thinking of a new exodus? Certainly the Gospels refer to Jesus as the way? And understanding ourselves in a new exodus may remind us that we live in a continuing story of God's work with the world. Regardless of what we think about a possible new exodus, the fact remains that God's people have continually sojourned. UCLA scholar Robert Alter asserts that the Exodus narrative revolves around three spaces:

✓ *Egypt – the place of bondage*
✓ *The Wilderness – the place where freedom will be realized.*

✓ *The Promised Destination – A land that remains beyond the horizon.*[33]

> Using Alter's three spaces, how would you describe your sojourn?

....

....

....

QUESTIONS

➢ Compare the beginnings of Matthew, Luke and John to Mark. What do you make of Mark's straightforward beginning?

➢ Review the session individual questions. Ask for participants to share.

➢ As a group take Stephen Prothero's biblical literacy test. How did you fair?

➢ Review the common mission or task the group decided on and discuss its execution.

---

[33] Alter, Robert. The Five Books of Moses: A Translation with Commentary.

CHAPTER 14

The Power of Touch

SCRIPTURE

Read Matthew 9:18-26

FIRST THINGS

Researchers at many universities are studying the power of touch. The University of Miami has its own Touch Research Institute. MIT has the Laboratory for Human and Machine Haptics, aka *the Touch Lab*. Scholars have shown how touch helps infants grow, reduces disease and controls pain. We've all experienced this power of touch. It seems that MRIs may confirm, after all, the power of mom's touch on scraped knees.

> How has touch made a difference in your life?

STUDY

The Bible recounts several stories of people wanting to touch Jesus. In Matthew 8 Jesus touched a leper and Peter's mother-in-law, and they were both healed. This gives way to the power in the touch of Jesus elsewhere. A bleeding woman, the townspeople of Gennesaret (Matthew 14), and even as Mark 6 says *all* the towns and villages give evidence to Jesus' touch. In fact, this bleeding woman appears in each of the Synoptic

Gospels. It's a powerful testimony to her faith. Just consider what she's against:

- ✓ *She is never named, and thus has a sketched identity.*
- ✓ *She is bleeding. In fact, she has been bleeding for 12 years.*
- ✓ *She is out and about in the crowd – which means she is also breaking the law and unclean in the eyes of the law.*
- ✓ *She has no money. Matthew, who is usually good with detail fails to state what both Mark and Luke record that she had "spent all she had," on various doctors.*

Despite her odds, she reaches out to Jesus. Apparently, she never worries about what to ask Jesus. She isn't preparing a big speech or rationale to be healed. After twelve years, her actions this day seem to indicate she also isn't concerned with her status or thoughts of embarrassment. Rather, she simply has a conviction that if she even touches the clothes of Jesus, she would be healed.

While her conviction is faithful and admiring, it nonetheless helps to spark unusual convictions as well. Is there magic in the touch of Jesus? Is there something to seeing Jesus' face in a grilled cheese sandwich?[34] Could seeing an image of Jesus in a cloud or shadow make a difference? Might touching something like Jesus' burial shroud spark greater faith? Some people put a lot of emphasis on stigmatas, icons, and garlands. I've met someone who just might be classified as obsessed with the Shroud of Turin. Is there merit in his obsession? Is there anything to all the religious trinkets that sat for years on my grandmother's mantle?

---

[34] See http://abcnews.go.com/Entertainment/WolfFiles/story?id=307227&page=1 for some interesting thoughts.

> Touching Jesus became ritualized, as do so many things we do. What are some of your rituals?

....

....

....

One year in Haiti with a group of students we spent a day moving rocks from one place to another. We were building a third story addition to an orphanage. The work was intense especially in the heat of the day. The orphanage faced a cliff as well which meant any small slip could have been detrimental. There's no doubt the orphanage needed space and I had a bunch of college students willing to take the risk and move the rock. But I needed to expose these same students to a different kind of risk.

So the next day, I took them to a hospital in Delmas. They care for children, mostly babies, hospitalized from HIV and TB. Some of the scenes are obviously tragic and tough to witness. However, the hospital does a great job at making many of these kids feel good, despite their time is short. Indeed, most are dying. Actually there wasn't a lot of work a group of college students could do. There were no rocks to move. The rooms didn't need new paint. There was no arbitrary mission work to be done like so many mission farms provide.

So, we just held the kids. We rocked them back and forth. We gave them piggyback rides and we fed the babies. We brushed their hair, held their hands and played peak-a-boo.

This nameless, poor, law breaking, bleeding lady who touches Jesus, who sees some power in just his presence, is a risk taker. For her, his touch is more than ritual. It's not about his clothes or any artifact. It's riskier. It may not sound like a risk to go and touch the clothes of Jesus. Just like it might not sound like a risk to hold a dying baby. But they are equally fraught with danger. There's nothing safe about getting attached to a child who you know will die. Why would anyone want to loose someone they love? Likewise, there's nothing safe about getting attached to Jesus. We can move rocks all day and get our hands dirty. But, if we don't reach out and touch the dying or the hurting then we are, as Reinhold Niebuhr claimed, "too cautious to be a Christian." [35]

> Renowned 20th century theologian Reinhold Niebuhr said, "the whole Christian adventure is frustrated continually not so much by malice as by cowardice and reasonableness." Think of how this may be true in your own life:

....

....

....

Just to set the record straight you should know the woman wasn't healed because she touched Jesus. Read the story again and see for yourself. By the time she actually touched Jesus she was already healed. Nonetheless, she touched Jesus, which is rather remarkable. It's remarkable because the Hebrew Bible takes great pain to stress that God is untouchable. Consider Exodus 19, which explains how Moses was to set up a boundary between Yahweh and the people. Sacredness to remain sacred

---

[35] Reinhold Niebuhr: Leaves from the notebook of a tamed cynic.

could not be penetrated. In Numbers 3, for instance, we read no one could approach the sanctuary. Thankfully this nameless woman had enough reason to reject such a bad idea. God was in her midst, so she took a gamble that paid off.

But what is most remarkable is that this bleeding woman didn't even realize she was healed. Trying to touch Jesus, she was mindlessly unaware of how God had already touched her.

> Share an experience when God has touched you:

....

....

....

QUESTIONS

➤ How can you, as a group of disciples, make use of the work of MIT's Touch Lab.

➤ What do you make of the boundaries of the holy and sacred found in the Hebrew Bible? Do traditions or superstitions influence your actions in church?

CHAPTER 15

Sightseeing

SCRIPTURE

Read Mark 10:46-52

FIRST THINGS

A student at NC State, Keith Burns, designed some t-shirts I saw at a recent conference. They referenced 2 Corinthians 5:7 "we live by faith, not by sight." Unlike most Christian shirts, his artwork is original. Take a look:

Now take a second and look at the image again, but upside down. At first glance we read "by faith." But when you see the image upside down you read, "not sight."

> Although we are called to live by faith, why do you think the Bible makes so many references to sight?

_____

_____

STUDY

The Bible utilizes sight in many ways. We worship a God who sees. And often our sight, from the Biblical perspective, deals with wisdom and intelligence. That's why blindness is exemplified regularly. Here's just a sampling:

    ✓   *I was eyes to the blind, and feet to the lame. (Job 29:15)*

    ✓   *The Lord opens the eyes of the blind. (Psalm 146:8)*

    ✓   *One who turns a blind eye will get many a curse. (Proverbs 28:27)*

    ✓   *The eyes of the blind shall be opened. (Isaiah 35:5)*

More often than not the Scripture refers to blindness as a way of explaining perspective rather than a medical condition. Who is usually considered blind in the Scriptures are those who fail to see what's to be seen, rather than having a physical limitation that prevents sight. Consider this passage from Ecclesiastes:

> *Whatever my eyes desired I did not keep from them; I kept my heart from no pleasure, for my heart found pleasure in all my toil, and this was my reward for all my toil ... Then I saw that wisdom excels folly as light excels darkness. The wise have eyes in their head, but fools walk in darkness. Yet I perceived that the same fate befalls all of them (2:10,13-14)*

> Consider some times when you have been blind. When have you not realized the whole situation?

Good sight (or insight) isn't as obvious as it would seem. We suffer from a healthcare crisis today because smart people don't act smart. Physicians are worried and pay high prices for malpractice insurance. Clinic managers attempt to reduce the time doctors spend with patients because they see the bottom line. Health insurance companies require patients to fight and appeal for coverage, even though they pay high premiums. Not to mention the uninsured, the under insured and the uninsurable. Do we have a healthcare crisis or war? Bullets are flying from every direction.

I must admit I also get sick when my own doctor orders a CT scan. Chances are my health insurance will not cover the test and I also get frustrated walking into elaborate hospitals adorned with glass walls, waterfalls and marble floors. I can't help but think my CT bill offsets the leather couches, flat-screens and other goodies I would rather not buy.

After it's all said and done, along with my bill I get a survey. We're asked to rate our doctors. Now we have the opportunity to grade their performance. Which of course means physicians also have the temptation of doing what is right versus doing what the patient desires. Sometimes their ethical convictions win. But we also know of plenty of ambivalent professionals that give patients everything they request.

It's not obvious that we are blind to this. We can see plenty of different things. But perhaps its best to see things differently. That's what happened to me when my wife had two surgeries at the Mayo Clinic. It was a very eye-opening experience to say the least. The secret to the Mayo Clinic is the fact that their physicians are salaried. There is no incentive for a Mayo Clinic doctor to perform medical procedures other than that of helping the patient. Most everywhere else the doctors get paid per procedure. And at the Mayo Clinic every patient is treated as a whole person working with a team of physicians. No diagnosis is given in isolation. The Mayo Clinic assumes that what happens to one part of the body may influence the conditions of another part. So, ironically, differing specialist actually talk to one another. I also recall physicians willing to spend hours – not minutes – answering our every question.

The Mayo Clinic is unique. It's a model difficult to replicate, which is another reason why it has its critics. But when our eyes are opened, not only do we see, we also realize we were once blind. Blindness, metaphorically, is never flattering. No one wants to be in the dark. It's like the awkwardness of the knuckle touch meeting the high five. Likewise, I find healthcare now a bit awkward in light of seeing how it can be done at the Mayo Clinic.

> How has your own blindness to a situation caused awkwardness?

....

....

....

Blindness causes embarrassment and awkwardness because we fail. Sometimes we fail to see because we are lazy. Sometimes we overlook. Sometimes we ignore. Sometimes we are hypocritical. Diana Butler Bass, the church historian, writes, "part of the problem of contemporary Christianity is that it has not been what it says it is. In the West it seems hypocritical and phony; its words and actions collide."[36]

---

[36] Bass, Diana Butler. A People's History of Christianity: The other side of the story.

> Share some times when you have seen, experienced, or played a part in the church's hypocrisy.

....

....

....

The Jewish world at the time of Jesus expected the Messiah to bring sight to the blind. Literally. And Jesus did on multiple occasions. One such time was on the Jericho road where Jesus encountered a blind beggar named Bartimaeus. Just before Jesus restores Bartimaeus' sight, James and John, two of his disciples, asked Jesus for an elevation in their status. They asked Jesus for positions of power and distinction in the afterlife. It wasn't out of the ordinary. We see the likes of Joel Osteen and Creflo Dollar preach a prosperity Gospel, asking special favors of God as well.

Prosperity gospel isn't reserved for the religious. Look at Jintao in China, Mugabe in Zimbabwe, and Kim Jong-Il in North Korea. They live the high life and seek favoritism as their people suffer under their brutality. We live this locally as well. When's the last time you passed by a "school of distinction," or a "top 100 hospital." Does it matter if Harvard and Princeton battle for the top school? We rank best college towns, best places to retire, best law firms, and even best party schools. So, the favors of James and John aren't hard to imagine.

But the favor Bartimaues asks of Jesus ranks above the rest. Jesus knew he was blind. His condition was more than obvious. He was shouting out to the Messiah "Jesus, Son of David, have mercy." Those around criticized him. In fact, he probably took a severe tongue-lashing, perhaps even from James and John. And when Jesus asked Bartimaues "what do you want me to do to you?" imagine the response of James and John who had just asked for everything. Bartimaues had Jesus' attention. He certainly could have asked for anything. But he only asked for what he needed saying, "Rabbi, I want to see." Don't you find it amusing that it is the blind man who has enough insight to ask for what he truly needs? It was the blind man who knew, like David in the story of Israel, what was "right in the sight of the Lord." (see 1 Kings 15).

> If God asked you "what do you want from me," what kinds of things would you ask for? Would they be right in his eyes?

....

....

....

QUESTIONS

> There are a lot of reasons why the Mayo Clinic is a successful model for healthcare. They have a niche, they approach the body as holistic and so forth. Discuss possible traits of seeing a situation differently and thus making a difference?

> James and John wanted to be the best. This is pervasive in our culture. What wisdom does the simple life of Bartimaues teach?

CHAPTER 16

Listening to the Ice

SCRIPTURE

Read Mark 12:28-34

FIRST THINGS

Dr. Oz tells us that ears are the only part of the body that grow with age. I don't watch Dr. Oz much and my own doctor shrills at his name. More importantly, I don't know anything about anatomy, but what he says sounds good. Unless you already have big ears.

> What do you think your ears have to do with faith?

....

....

....

STUDY

Once flying into Minneapolis I had the chance to see hundreds of lakes frozen over by ice. From the tiny window I could see trucks driving back and forth and shanties on the ice. Being from the south, it was hard for me to understand this Minnesotan pastime. It's still puzzling for me to consider open fires, power augers, heavy trucks and lots of beer as being suitable for ice-covered lakes. For quite awhile I assumed that these Minnesotans were just cracked. But in Kansas of all places, I learned otherwise. I happened to run into three mostly inebriated loggers from

Minnesota in a hotel lobby one evening and their very thick wild north accents lured me in. I thought finally I could catch a glimpse into the mysterious world of ice fishing. And you betcha I did. Oh yah, come to find out, the real secret to ice fishing, I learned, was to *listen to the ice.*

Until then, I didn't know ice talked.

Surprisingly, they are right. Like the fox in Aesop's fable that listened to the ice, these Minnesotans use sonar and other sophisticated listening equipment. Sonar is used to aid the navy, everyday boaters in shallow waters and even biologist to listen to the whales. We use ultrasound to see pictures of babies in the womb and take pictures of the heart and its vessels. It turns out that sound is pretty sophisticated, even for drunken Minnesotan anglers.

> How much do you rely on sound?

....

....

....

As we have discovered in previous rounds, the Hebrew Bible had many laws. Perhaps up to 613 laws are recorded in the Torah.[37] So, it's not hard to imagine why Jewish leaders asked Jesus which law was the most important. When asked what the greatest commandment was, Jesus answered "the first is, 'Hear, O Israel: the Lord our God, the Lord is one; you shall love the Lord your God with all your heart, and with all your soul, with all your mind, and all your strength.' The second is this, 'You shall love your neighbor as yourself' (Mark 12:29-31)." The first

---

[37] Just Google Mitzvot.

commandment that Jesus refers is called the *shema*, which in Hebrew means to hear. The people of Israel were summoned to "Hear, O Israel: the Lord our God, the Lord is one (Deuteronomy 6:4)."

While *shema* means to hear, it also carries with it an anticipated acceptance. Hearing isn't quite enough. We must also listen. Alternatively, the *shema* serves as a confession or recognition of faith. That recognition is born in hearing. By contrast consider all the times you've heard Christian altar calls: "Come forward tonight and *tell* the Lord you love him." Despite the fact that the altar call is never found in the Bible, lots of churches use this as a time for new followers to *speak* of their faith – to acknowledge salvation. But here Jesus told the scribe to *hear*.

Likewise, consider prayer. How often is prayer spoken? The Quakers and Amish, however, exemplify that prayer can be a matter of listening to God as well.

> What does it mean for you to hear in a spiritual sense?

....

....

....

It's not by accident that hearing is part of the greatest commandment. Listening is essential in all of life. Faithful discipleship, according to Jesus actually requires listening. You can hear with your ears but you can only listen with your heart. There's a difference. It's the latter that is most important. John's Gospel speaks to this sound when we read, "in the beginning was the Word, and the Word was with God, and the Word was God (John 1:1)." It's as if Jesus could have just as easily told the scribe "hear the Word."

> What does it mean to hear the Word?

....

....

....

Popularized recently by Thomas Keating centering prayer is an admirable technique that requires diligent patience and spiritual fitness. This is but one of many ways to center your prayers:

- ✓ *Find a comfortable room with as much silence as possible.*
- ✓ *Relax yourself, with good posture, and focus on a spiritual word, like love, life, spirit, or something of the sort.*
- ✓ *Turn your hands up as they rest on your knees and close your eyes and try to clear your mind.*
- ✓ *Whenever your mind wanders and you can't focus on nothingness, recall the word you chose and try to re-center.*
- ✓ *Do this for twenty minutes.*

I believe centering prayer is incredibly dynamic in its attempt to listen to God because it never underestimates our need to hear. Most every time I try centering prayer I become lost in my own chaos, my own worries, and my own thoughts. It's all about me. However, when it's done effectively and I'm true to just listening to the stillness of God, I can become lost in God's silence. It's then that I hear. Like the Psalmist, centering prayer helps me to be still and thus know God (46:10).

> Trying centering prayer and share your thoughts below.

....

....

....

QUESTIONS

➢ In this round I mentioned the listening prayers of both the Amish and Quakers. Find out more about these traditions and their differing methods of prayer.

➢ There are many contemplative ways to pray that utilize silence. As a group, spend an extended period of time together in silent prayer.

➢ Review the common mission or task the group decided on and discuss its execution.

CHAPTER 17

Something Stinks

SCRIPTURE

Read Genesis 8

FIRST THINGS

Smell is very controlling. Marketing firms often suggest their clients manipulate the smells of their businesses to influence customers.

> How has smell influenced you?

STUDY

In a moment of weakness, one day I purchased a bag of cinnamon scented pinecones. On the car ride home, I kept asking myself "who buys pinecones?" Because the cinnamon scent reminds me of Christmas this brief jolt to my past opened my wallet. I know some churches that intentionally bake their communion bread so visitors and members will likewise have positive emotions. Ever considered how every Habitat for Humanity site smells alike. New construction has the aroma of progress. Funeral homes all smell alike as well (but not with the scent of progress). Anytime I visit the doctor's office and wash my hands, the sterile smell of the soap follows me home. In fact, we spend a lot of time covering bad smells.

A few years back I took a team of college students to the Baja coast of Mexico. Here we organized a benefit for an AIDS house and worked with a church in a small rural village near the coast. The church was growing and needed to expand. They had the ability in their village to build a new building and so they did. But, for our satisfaction, they saved installing a new septic tank for the American mission team. The plan was to dig a 12x12 pit at least eight feet deep. I'm no soil expert, but the region was rather arid. Perhaps more like a desert: Clayish, hard, rocky and dry. Let's just say it wasn't easy.

It wasn't until the third day that we began to make some progress with our shovels. The soil started softening and so we worked faster. The earth had loosened up and mud was flying everywhere. We were all covered and filthy. Then the mud turned to slop and we discovered an open pipe spewing right into our pit. Unfortunately … regrettably … we had broken their first septic line. We were all covered in caca.

The village was saturated with stench. Like a NASCAR pit crew several locals ran toward the pit with bags of lime. Which only made the smell worse as white particles of wretchedness floated for days. The smell was unfathomable. It lingered in our clothes, in our sleeping bags and lodged with our luggage. The smell was so intense Felipe, the pastor, even decided to preach on the decaying smell of Lazarus who had been dead for four days (John 11). As a mission team our intent was to bring life and hope, but instead we had busted open the smell of death.

> Smells let us know when things are right or wrong. What smells bad in your own faith journey? What smells good?

....

....

....

The Hebrew Bible speaks of pleasing God with the aromas of burnt offerings. The Hebrew word we usually read as 'pleasing' is *nihoah*. The word is better translated as 'fragrant' and it is always connected with sacrifice. The word is also most definitely a play on the name Noah because he was the first to discover this oddity and influence over God. We know there is no doubt that smells influence us. But have you ever considered that smells influence God? Noah did.

With Noah's construction of an altar and his burnt offerings, he set in motion what Hebrew scholar John Kselman calls the "postdiluvian system divine of service." [38] Once Noah discovered humans could influence God, an entire system of sacrifices arose. A sacrifice could on one hand show praise to God, but most often it was used instead to please God and make amends. Agriculturally speaking, it was important for the God of wind and rain to be patient and kind. Please God, the ancients believed, and therefore God will return the favor. So in such fashion, Israel offered at least five postdiluvian sacrifices. They are found in the first chapters of Leviticus:

✓ *Burnt Offering – act of forgiveness for unintentional sins.*
✓ *Grain Offering – thanking God for general provisions.*

---

[38] Kselman, John. Genesis. Harper's Bible Commentary.

✓   *Peace Offering – communal meal offering of thanks.*

✓   *Sin Offering – confessional act of cleansing.*

✓   *Guilt Offering – act of reparation and restitution.*

While we might think of burnt offerings as cultic[39], we should take a serious look at how we too try to please others, including God. Men wear cologne and women wear perfume to please others – not themselves. In fact we have a rather sophisticated ritual of mating. Other modern day rituals include applying for college and getting a job. We adapt to the standard accepted practices in most of life. "Even hipsters are subject to following a prescribed and accredited course."[40]

Israelite rituals were originally designed to influence God, but like any ritual they could become idolatrous in nature. It's always good to be careful not to worship the ritual itself. This may sound obvious, but researchers have found even gamblers don't like to win. Instead they would rather continue to gamble. Idolatry like most addictions forms innocently and develops blindly over time. The addiction of religious fundamentalism was a continual motif in the experiences of Jesus. Scribes, Pharisees, and other Jewish sects of his day were guilty of taking the law and codes to the extreme. And we all know people who likewise love the church more than God.

We also know people who worship doctrine. Doctrine worship stinks. Doctrine worship smells bad because it presets one's understanding of God.[41] For example many Christians take Jesus' words in John 14:6 as a systematic theological treatise instead of perhaps an invitation to

---

[39] A cult is simply a new religious group. Often the term in used in a pejorative way to mean a group that is dangerous or destructive.

[40] McCracken, Brett. Hipster Christianity: When church and cool collide.

[41] Hirsch, Alan & Debra. Untamed: Reactivating a missional form of discipleship.

discipleship. He said, "I am the way, the truth, and the life. No one comes to the Father except through me." As a doctrine, it becomes a rule of exclusiveness. Many use this verse to limit a person's relationship with God. I understand this verse, however, as a very inclusive verse where Jesus is celebrating that God's way is the way of Jesus – the way of life and truth.

Another example of doctrine worship is what is commonly called Bible believing. Bible believing smells bad because Christians aren't called to believe the bible. Paradoxically those who are Bible believers read the same Bible that makes no such claim on itself. Instead, we are challenged and invited to believe God ... God alone. Bible believing is a modern doctrine, only developed after the advent of the printing press. Otherwise, we would have scroll believers. And not only that, with all of the possible Biblical translations available, which Bible do Bible believers believe?[42]

Turn in your Bible to Mark 16. Do you believe in Mark 16:1-8 or Mark 16:1-20? This last section in Mark's gospel is absent from early Greek manuscripts. A similar occurrence is found in John 8. Because the Bible is a collection of different ancient works, every English translation has its difficulties. Similar problems arise in the Hebrew Bible. Some Bibles include adjustments found in the Dead Sea Scrolls and most also use the Greek version of the Hebrew Bible, called the Septuagint, as a guide.

Actually what we consider the Bible is really quite messy. Simply put, the Bible isn't God. Though the Bible invites us to be smitten by God's

---

[42] Cox, Harvey. The Future of Faith.

love.[43] Jesus didn't give sight to the blind, heal the sick, preach peace and love, suffer and die for us to worship doctrine or bible believe. He didn't rise from death for us to fight over translations. Rather, the Bible is a narrative that reveals the immeasurable love of God. Jesus doesn't call us to take up a set of principles and presets. He calls us to love.

> Reflect on some religious habits, rituals, or presets in your own life that get in the way of having a deeper relationship with God. Which of these can you wipe clean?

....

....

....

QUESTIONS

➤ As a group make a quick list of all the smells you have encountered just today. Discuss how these and other smells influence us.

➤ Review the session individual questions. Ask for participants to share.

➤ List examples of Christian beliefs that you think might smell bad? What commonalities did the group share?

---

[43] See Kenda Creasy Dean's Almost Christian: What the faith of our teenagers is telling the American church. Dean utilizes the term 'smitten' a lot in her work to emphasize how awe-struck we ought to be in response to God's love.

CHAPTER 18

You are the Equipment

SCRIPTURE

Read Acts 16:16-40

FIRST THINGS

Some of the most amazing people I know are hikers. And by amazing I mean patient. I don't know Kevin Gallagher, but he radiates amazement to me in his 2,200 mile Appalachian Trail hike video he posted on Vimeo. It took him six months to hike the famous trail. Yet he condensed his experience into a five-minute video. Six months...and I complain when the store only has three of its twenty-six lanes open. Abraham, the founder of the Jewish nation, "grew strong in his faith (Romans 4:20)" after waiting twenty some years for a son. And I exit the interstate and take a ten-mile detour to avoid a half-mile backup.

> Is there something you have devoted your life to in a way that is similar to Kevin Gallagher's sixth month trek?

....

....

....

STUDY

There are two basic ways that Christians can view time. *Chronos* is the type of time we measure. Think chronology as a way we count the seconds we can hold our breath and hours we can devote to Facebook.

Or think chronic as a type of medical condition that doesn't go away. Another way we can view time is by thinking in terms of *Kairos*.

Kairos is the right time.

Although Jesus hears Lazarus is very sick, he waits. In fact, Jesus waits two extra days before heading out to help. His response is anything but efficient. "When Jesus finally got there, he found Lazarus already four days dead (John 11:17 THE MESSAGE)."

I have a friend who seems to always be late for everything. She's missed flights, shown up late to classes and meetings and even started her wedding a bit late. This is despite the fact she sets all of her clocks ahead of time, but each with different times as to keep her unaware of the real time, and still ends up late to about everything. She takes a lot of time to manipulate time and as a result is mostly always in some way exploited by time. I'm convinced her strange behavior is an attempt to fight *chronos* and embrace *kairos*.

> You've been late to things. Jot down some things you've really been late for and share some of the related consequences.

In contrast to Jesus, and my time-crazed friend, Lazarus' sister Martha spares no time. Immediately she meets Jesus on the road as he approaches saying, "Lord, if you had been here, my brother would not have died (John 11:21)." Martha was thinking in terms of *chronos*. Jesus was thinking *kairos*. It's our own internal battle of *chronos* v. *kairos* that causes impatience. Like Martha, the people in Egypt were impatient with God. In fact, our impatience can be overwhelming.

> We've all grown impatient with God. Share a few times when you feel God could have intervened but didn't.

....

....

....

I spent one Christmas Eve curled up in a small corner of a tight waiting room with about thirty other people while my wife was in ICU. Each of us in the waiting room was struggling with our particular pain and grief. One family occupied the opposite corner. Their eighteen year-old family member, Kirk, wrecked his motorcycle. The pressure in his brain couldn't be stabilized, internal bleeding was out of control, and his vital organs were failing. He was dying. This is when minutes feel like days and hours feel like years. Time for everyone in the room was standing still.

Chronos was in control.

Then, as if it came from nowhere, I heard a melody from the opposite corner of the waiting room. "Silent night, holy night." Within seconds, the entire waiting room chimed in "all is calm, all is bright." A chill covered my body then as it still does today. The waiting room, full of anxiety and stress experienced a calming peace that Christmas Eve. In hurt and sorrow, about the only thing we could do was sing, as if time stood still in a mysterious tribute to God's glory.

Kairos arrived.

Similarly, Paul and Silas in the book of Acts were struggling as prisoners. Albeit the circumstances, about the only thing they could do was sing. And they did. The Acts story ends in a miracle when their singing causes the earth to shake and the prison doors to open and even the saving and baptism of a guard's entire family (see Acts 16). Kirk died Christmas day. I am not sure how many miracles his family witnessed as a result of his life, but I do know his family's devotion to God in their time of grief was mighty miraculous.

> Read Ecclesiastes 3:1-8. What time is it?

Patience concerns *kairos* time. Impatience is a matter of *chronos*. Our impatience over both pity and important things exemplifies our own selfish nature. I grow impatient waiting in line because of own my personal agenda. I grow impatient with traffic jams, the lines for roller coasters, at the DMV, and whenever I have to wait. It's most always about me. However, clothing yourself with patience (Colossians 3:12) ... throwing on the hiking gear ... twists our agenda toward the concern of others. That's a matter of *kairos*.

> Give some examples of how you can shift your own impatience toward an attitude of patience.

QUESTIONS

➤ The Acts 16 text exposes a lot more than just patience. Make a list of all the ideas, concepts, and teachings the group can glean from this passage.

➤ If time and location allows, try sitting as a group in silence. Keep your eyes open so you can look at one another. Determine by body language who is becoming impatient the quickest. Discuss how this exercise eventually challenges you.

➤ Review the common mission or task the group decided on and discuss its execution.

WORKS CITED

Alter, Robert. The Five Books of Moses: A Translation with Commentary. WW Norton & Company. 2004.

Aristide, Jean-Bertrand. Eyes of the Heart: Seeking a path for the poor in the age of globalization. Common Courage Press. 2000.

Bass, Diana Butler. A People's History of Christianity: The other side of the story. HarperOne. 2009.

Bell, Rob. Love Wins: A Book About Heaven, Hell, and the Fate of Every Person Who Ever Lived. HarperOne. 2011.

Boff, Leonardo. Spirituality and Politics. From Liberation Theology by Cadorette, Giblin, Legge and Snyder. Orbis Books. 1992.

Book of Common Prayer. The Church Hymnal Corporation. 2001.

Chan, Francis. Erasing Hell: What God said about eternity, and the things we made up. David C. Cook. 2011.

Claiborne, Shane & Chris Haw. Jesus for President: Politics for Ordinary Radicals. Zondervan 2008.

Cox, Harvey. The Future of Faith. HarperOne. 2009.

Crossan, John Dominic. God & Empire: Jesus against Rome, then and now. HarperCollins. 2007.

Dean, Kenda Creasy. Almost Christian: What the Faith of Our Teenagers is Telling the American Church. Oxford University Press

de Becker, Gavin. The Gift of Fear and Other Survival Signals that Protect Us From Violence. Dell. 1999

ESV Study Bible. Crossway Bibles. 2001.

Flynn, Mary. As more Oakland youth join the sex trade, law enforcement explores alternatives to incarceration. Oakland North. March 13, 2010.

Foster, Richard. A Year with God: Living Out the Spiritual Disciplines. HarperOne. 2009.

Grove, Andrew. Only the Paranoid Survive: How to Exploit the Crisis Points That Challenge Every Company. Crown Business. 1999.

The Harper Collins Study Bible, Revised Edition. Harper-Collins Publishers. 2006.

Hirsch, Alan & Debra. Untamed: Reactivating a missional form of discipleship. BakerBooks. 2010.

Honey, Charles. Could you live like Jesus for a year? This pastored tried. USA Today, January 2, 2009.

Kselman, John. Genesis. Harper's Bible Commentary. HarperCollins. 1988.

McCracken, Brett. Hipster Christianity: When church and cool collide. BakerBooks. 2010.

Mother Teresa and Brian Kolodiejchuk. Come be My Light. Image. 2009.

Mueller, John. Clare of Assisi: The Letters to Agnes. Liturgical Press. 2003.

The New Interpreter's Study Bible. Abingdon Press. 2003.

Niebuhr, Reinhold. Leaves from the notebook of a tamed cynic. Westminster/John Knox Press. 1929

Powell, Kara and Chap Clark. Sticky Faith: Everyday ideas to build lasting faith in your kids. Zondervan. 2011.

Prothero, Stephen. Religious Literacy: What Every American Needs to Know-- And Doesn't. HarperOne. 2008.

Shachtman, Tom. Rumspringa: To Be or Not To Be Amish. North Point Press. 2007.

Sutton, Robert. Good Boss, Bad Boss: How to Be the Best... and Learn from the Worst. Business Plus. 2010.

Witherington, Ben. Blog: http://benwitherington.com

Wright, N.T. Simply Christian: Why Christianity makes sense. HarperSanFrancisco. 2006.

Made in the USA
Charleston, SC
14 February 2013